The Collection

In this debut collection, *Red Fox Runs: Poems 2011-2016* takes
the reader through the highs and lows of a Millennial's first five
years living in New York City. The poems explore themes of
self-identity, failure and reinvention. Others reflect on emerging
adulthood topics such as the end of youth and finding purpose.

The Red Fox symbolizes aspiration and applies to anyone
desirous of achieving greatness in their lifetime.

Culture can't thrive without disruptions.

RED FOX RUNS / Joseph Adam Lee

Poems: 2011-2016

Red Fox Runs Press
New York, New York

RED FOX RUNS PRESS
909 3RD AVENUE
#127
NEW YORK, NEW YORK 10150

An imprint of The Rebel Within

Publisher's Note

This is a work of fiction. Names, characters, places and incidents either are
the product of the author's imagination or are used fictitiously. Any resemblance
to actual persons, living or dead, business establishments, events, or locales is
entirely coincidental.

The publisher does not have any control over and does not assume any
responsibility for authorship for author or third-party Web sites or their content.

Acknowledgments
Content Editor: Sam Hughes
Cover & Layout Design: Eleni Rouketa

Contact Information
Email: joe@therebelwithin.com
Websites: www.josephadamlee.com
Instagram: @joseph.adam.lee

Library Of Congress Cataloging-In-Publication Data
Lee, Joseph Adam. 1986-
Red Fox Runs: Poems 2011-2016 / Joseph Adam Lee.

LCCN: 2016960854

ISBN: 978-0-692-80086-7 (Paperback)
ISBN: 978-1-946673-34-3 (Hardcover)
ISBN: 978-1-946673-96-1 (e-book)
ISBN: 978-1-946673-35-0 (Audiobook)

to *Evariste Bisson*

Table of Contents

Red Fox Runs

Reinvention is a choice.
Don't let it pass you by.

When the Running Stops

(Youth's Urgency)

You won't even know it until it hits you.
Your sense of invincibility will wane.
The vaguest sense of uncertainty will strike you.

It will most likely happen after a long late evening.
You'll hate everything about that morning:
the environment
the people
the stuff...
You may even hate yourself.

Take this as a gift,
an awakening.
You'll drab throughout the day
Watching YouTube videos
and eating Macaroni and Cheese.
But, even in a hung-over state, reflect.

Happiness is near.
The sky will look different tomorrow.
The streets will vibrate .
Colors will become vibrant again.

Everything can change.

This goodness will seem foreign.
It may scare you.
But that's when you have
the opportunity to make a choice.

You may ignore it: maybe you're not ready.
But, if you want change,
when you hear air whisper truth into your ear,
then you'll know it's time to change.
Change is okay.

So do it already.

Just fucking do it!
Otherwise, you're wasting time.

Distractions are easy.
And you can run on their track for as long as you want.
Run barefoot if you'd like.
Pound your feet deeply into the gravel.
Hell, become part of the terrain.
It's only you that can stop.

So stop running.
Stop!
While you have the chance.

Journey

Your journey is a lifetime spent
searching, questioning and reaching for realization.
The goal is always subjective.
You'll arrive where you are supposed to.
Instincts will help push your boundaries,
and you'll become
good
better
greater
than your former self.

Personally, I'm enticed by
the endless road of possibilities.
I'm keen on taking adventures.
I don't believe in holding roots.
Stability hinders me.

Complacency leaves no room for discovery.

My fire, it burns, searing through my veins
and arteries creating unexpected chills
as the blood passes through my organs.
Inspiration is not planned,
but sprung upon us by spontaneity
coming for a chance meeting,
a thought
a picture
a sound
a feeling.

Search within yourself, find something,
and set out on the unexpected journey.

Park Bench

Just before work, I walk past a park bench.
It's green, usually empty, and
many people, like me, give it little notice.

I wonder if the bench feels ignored.
I wonder if a bench can be lonely.

It seems like it is in a good spot,
situated on the southeastern side of Central Park.
Maybe people sit and share their lives on it.
They might discuss the recent headlines
in the Times or the Wall Street Journal.
They may retell stories that they
haven't thought of in a while.
Maybe a budding romance has formed,
or a begrudged man has
broken his lover's heart there.

Possibly, someone has found closure after
visiting the bench.

Once, in the middle of the night,
I saw a man lie across the bench.
The bench mustn't mind any of this.
It has its purpose
as a soundboard
as an unexpected friend
as a location to start anew
as... a home.

I don't know if I'll ever have a free moment
to sit on the park bench.
I'm thinking I might move out of this town soon.

But I know where the bench is; it'll stay...always,
stable,
empty of emotion, but full of responsibility;
every bit alone, but certainly among company.

It can make you envious.
I really should get a cup of coffee and
catch up with a good friend,
maybe share some thoughts while sitting
on the park bench.

*If you offer someone
a piece of stale toast,
they won't eat it,
but if you slap some
peanut butter on it
they probably will.*

Writer's Rant

Sometimes I hate writing.
It's a burden.
It reminds me that my mind moves too fast
and I can't catch up.

Time doesn't allow you to capture everything

But I will try.
I've become consumed by it.
I'm addicted to memory.
I never want to miss out.
Even if it's nothing.
Even if it needn't be recalled.
I want to keep it.
Who knows?
Maybe it'll help me later on.
Maybe it'll help me figure out what I
want to say
should say
could say.

But I will try.
I try to capture it.
Because if I don't, it's gone.
So many people take that for granted.
I don't.
I do everything I possibly can.
Every scribbled note is precious.
Every sentence kept.
Every word.
All of it.

But I will try.
I will try to remember.

Chilly Nights Make for Silent Sights

It was freezing in line.
Well, not freezing
but cold enough, you know?
Uncomfortable,
but not a cold that hurts.
Regardless, it was cold.

I didn't want to be there.
I really didn't, but it was Saturday
and I had nothing better to do.
Well, actually, I had plenty to do,
but I wanted to hang out with Brad and Jasper.
Stacy was there too.
She was smoking. I shared a drag.
I wanted to impress her
and everyone knew that,
even Stacy.

JP showed up. He's the club's promoter.
JP was fat, and for some reason
that really annoyed me.
He had been working at Suite 36 for 4 years.
4 years of promoting a club to boring people.
JP was boring but everyone wanted to be his friend.
Hell, even I tried to be his friend:
I wanted to get inside already!
Did I mention it was cold out?
Well, not that cold.

I felt boring,
also, kind of lame,
standing there and waiting to get into a club
that reeked of more lameness.
We had been drinking for over 4 hours.
I was at a good point. I didn't want to drink anymore.
I felt like I had been battling the bottle lately,
and Brad and Jasper were in the same boat.
Stacy, I wasn't sure about her.

She seemed sober.
I had only hung out with her a few times,
maybe 4 at the most.
I thought she was as radiant as ever.
I didn't tell her that, but Jasper and Brad knew
I thought about her in that way.
I sort of wished they didn't.
We reached the front of the line,
and two large black men stood in front of us.
It cost $35 to get into the club.
That was bullshit!
We had already blown $50 each that night.
I asked my new friend, JP, to let us in for free.
He lowered the entry fee to $20 dollars.
Fuck JP!
He's a douche bag.
I was jealous of him.
He had three girls on him, kissing him.
I wished Stacy was on me.
I wished any girl was on me.

JP smiled like a seal when we left.
There was no way we were paying $20 dollars.
There was no way we wanted to go into the club.
Maybe if we hadn't met JP we might have paid.
But then again I'm glad we didn't
because then we would have felt ripped off.
I wanted to just go back to
Jasper and Brad's place and talk.
I wanted Stacy to come too.
She wasn't as old as us, but her mind was.
That's what I liked about her,
but I could never tell her that.

I wanted to talk to anyone.
Well, except for JP
because, like I said, he's a douche bag.
What did I want to talk about?
Things
Things that mattered.

I'm not sure what they were
or would have been,
but I knew we would find them.
Either that, or something would find us.

We didn't talk.
We went into the cab, we went to another bar,
we blew another $50 bucks,
we blacked out and woke up the next morning.
I was disappointed.
We should have just stayed in.

So after my head stopped pounding
and I texted an apology to the bartender
for getting too drunk and being rude,
and Jasper left for the gym,
I sat with Brad.
We did exactly what I had wanted to do the night before:
we talked,
we just talked.
And after we finished,
I just wanted to talk more,
but we didn't,
we didn't talk anymore.

The Artist's Compromise

A cuddle sack of envy
based on the impending realization
that success won't come,
even when you are most desirous of it.
Yet, sensibility is something the artist must compromise.

How would anyone flourish without crazy intentions?

So be purposefully vulnerable, and create.

A mind wastes, unless it's creating.

The Man and the Yellow Subway Line

After another long spell of drinking
and trying to pull some skirt,
Rather victorious
Rather failing
I arrive at the N, Q or R subway stop
or simply, the Yellow Line.

I should have taken a cab,
but I spent too much on the booze.
Drinks for me
for my friends
for 'new' friends
for anyone, really, readily ready to drink with me.
Even worse,
I didn't know how much I spent.
Receipts, hurrahs printed on thin paper,
would remind me in the morning
of the gin and tonics
The IPAs
The Cabernets.
I should collect them and
ask the bartenders to sign them like baseball cards,
or have girls kiss them.
They'd leave ravishing pink lipstick marks.
Maybe another night.

The buzzing epicenter of the city is vacant.
Times Square wastes on its illumination
as I walk towards the subway's platform.
The bums mingle in peaceful harmony.
They stare at me.
Do I remind them of themselves
when they were my age?

Such a maze, this underworld.
That's when I see him,
the mosaic man on the subway station wall
still wearing his brown coat.

His top hat half-covers his tiled face,
like always.
His trademark orange scarf keeps him warm.
I ask him for the time.
It's a game we play
between the hours of 3:00 and 5:00 a.m.
He never responds.
I laugh at his motionless face.
I laugh with no one.
I leave the perpetual man concentrating on his watch.
I notice a new movie advertisement next to him.
I slap his flat shoulder.
I only need to remember three things once I find him:
Left, right, right.
The second right comes after the newsstand.
I wish I had a few bucks.
I would buy some chips or nuts,
something to preoccupy my sleep-deprived mind.

I wait for the underground space shuttle.
Once it comes, I enter the tube and sit.
I see sparks of propelling electricity
as the subway crosses the Queensboro Bridge
and
leaps over the East River.
I think,
another night,
and I can't wait to get home.

Finger Walker

If my fingers could speak, they would be screaming.
They would split open and bleed
with the anger known to many men.
Seeking nothing more than the chance,
No
The opportunity to be heard.
I guess that's why I write.
In the middle of a Friday night
with a beer to my right,
there's courage in writing.
And the best part is that it's free:
there are no restrictions, protocols
or restricted avenues.
I'm able to control, build and navigate the streets.
And, Hey!
If you don't like it,
get the fuck out of my way!

The avenue of broken dreams is a myth.

It's full of those who cut their fingers and bleed,
but are all too quick to cover them with bandages.
The glitz and the glam is an afterthought.
It isn't the goal.
Trust me on that.
The solidarity is enough to fill you
for a lifetime if you allow it.
It becomes muddled by entitlement,
and those expectations lead to the long road of misery.
I'll walk by it, but I won't let it overcome me.
I'd rather trip, then continue following that path.

Rockaway Sick Day

I held you.
You were so frail and I did not dare move.
No, there was no way.

You were like sand.
I feared loosening my grip.
I tightened and held you closer,
struggling against the sea's breeze.

If I had weakened my embrace,
I would have lost you.
You would have filtered through my arms,
breaking and crusting into a thousand pieces,
mixed with the endless toffee brown plane,
and awaiting your fatal fate
like a decrepit mercenary.

The ocean called to you.
The tide neared,
enticing you to escape.
Easily it could have flowed over you.
Gone
gone then, in a salty mixture.
The harshest takeover.
But I held tight, I held so tight.

I wasn't ready to let our love go.

A wounded beast cries on the inside.

We'll Keep Running As Long As You Keep Walking

(Blizzards of New York City)

I didn't mind the slushy terrain:
I grew up with white winters like this in Maine.
Oddly, I missed those mornings.
That day, I'll confess, I could have done without the wind.

"Suspended." They said.
"The trains won't be working."
"Everyone should take the day off."
I didn't have the day off.
No, the bastards needed to squeeze
every dime out of us.

It was 8:10 a.m.
I knew it would take me an hour to walk there.
I saw no people along the way,
but only yellow and green Martians
with reflective eyes,
and no hands... No one had hands.

The Queensboro Bridge was festive.
I wasn't the only one who had to go to work.
"Hey! Why is that train running?" A Martian pointed.
"Stop! let us get on, man!" Another Martian said.
It didn't stop.
It kept running.
It laughed at us.
The conductor looked out and said, "Suspended."

The train spat brown snow at us.
The globs looked like rocks,
but we weren't hurt by the dirty snow.
It reminded me of when
I would throw snowballs at my sister
before driving her to school.

I made it to the Manhattan side
and needed to walk 5 avenues before I made it to work.

As I neared, I saw people sprout
from the Lexington and 59th subway exit.
I said, "Hey, are the trains working now?"
Some girl looked at me like I was crazy.
I wasn't; I just wanted to know.
She said, "Yes, they started at 9:00am."

I looked at my watch.
It was 9:15am.
Shit, I thought.
I'm late for work.

Bum and Boil

The man was so distraught.
Maybe it was an act,
like the one the other beggars had mastered.

There's this girl, Shirley, who always
quacks about needing money for her kids.
I wonder where those kids are.
How is she able to walk
the trains all day without them?
How can she afford a babysitter?

I know, I know.
It's an act.
A daily job acting.
Homeless
and in need.

Scam artists are the best at abusing empathy.

They all have an angle,
but it's not too different from someone at a desk
avoiding responsibility but waiting for the handout.
Actually, the bums are pretty active
if you think about it.
They're doing something,
instead of looking at a clock
and waiting for the biweekly direct deposit.
My friends tell me I'm a fool
for wasting my money on them.
"You're supporting the scam, man."
Maybe I am.
Maybe?
I guess I'm soft.
I want to believe
that there is possibly some purity in it,
you know?
Is it that mind-blowing that this guy,
this embarrassed,

down on his luck,
vulnerable,
brave guy needs a fucking break?

We all need a break every once in a while.

We don't even realize it,
but some of us live our entire lives based on breaks.
This guy asks for a dollar.
I'll give him a five.
He looks at me.
I can't tell if it's part of the trick or not.
I don't really care.
I just hope that it helped.

Maybe it was the break he needed
to get back on his feet
to believe he has some self-worth
to know breaks happen
to give him a moment
to allow him to crack a fucking smile.

Anyhow, I don't want the money.
It'll only rot my soul in the end.
In some ways,
I'm giving myself a break.
So, in a way, the bum and I have the same shakedown.
If only there were more bums.
I should walk around with more
five-dollar bills in my pocket.

A Silent Joker in a Room Full of Laughter
(Corporate Meeting Milieu)

It begins again.
A room full of cackling idiots.
Each trying to prove that they're smart.
They say things they've said a hundred times before.
They grunt and pierce their eyes
with more obnoxious questions.
They place fingers under their chins.

Yeah, I do the same thing,
I act just like them.
We're all trying so hard,
but we don't know a friggin' thing.
It's all noise and whistles,
just like everything else that's going on lately.

"Who's this joker trying to tell me how to think?"
"This joker looks kind of young."
"Ah, he doesn't know anything – he's just a fucking kid."
"He doesn't know a damn thing."
"I don't agree with that, I think that you're off there."

"We're goin' ta make this joker squirm."

He's fine, - he's actually correct - but they don't care.
They're into it,
together and purposely closed-minded.

The joker tries to persuade the stubborn minds.
They're obstinate.
They shield themselves with fear,
but they'll never say that.
They'll weaken, but not as much as they should.

"He sounded smart, but he's got a long way to go."

I don't know why they do this.
I don't know why anyone does this.

What's the point.

I guess it's pride.
We all need to feel important.
We all need to feel witnessed.
I don't include myself,
I don't say a damn word,
and that's just the way they like it.

The minute the joker leaves,
the one who's smarter than the rest of us,
they'll act like they didn't need that.
They'll all act.
Just like everyone:
A world full of actors,
laughing at the people that aren't acting.

I'm ashamed to be an actor.
I'm ashamed that I laughed.
I'm ashamed that the jokers don't laugh.
If we just listened to the jokers, maybe we could progress,
maybe we wouldn't have to act,
but that isn't going to happen,
no, it's just not.

We won't let the jokers get the best of us,
but I'm rooting for the joker.
I hope that the joker makes them all stop laughing.
I hope that the joker makes them all shut the hell up.
I hope the joker makes them stop grunting, and that
their eyes widen.
I hope the joker stops them
from sitting on their stupid fingers.
I hope the joker wins.
I hope the joker has the last laugh.

Have I ever been wrong?
Well, I think the right question is:
Have I ever been right?
My answer would be, 'Rarely'.

Without

      growth

            there

                  is

                        nothing.

The Ledge Awaits Our Leap

There's a ledge,
you know?
I want to jump off it.
Maybe I'll fly or maybe I won't,
maybe I'll dive down deep into the abyss.
I know it'd be easier to walk back.
Yes, it'd be easier to return
to everything that is routine and natural,

Where I'm safe.

I can't!
If I did, I would be walking backwards
into my shadows.
When you fly, your shadow is under you.
It's only when you crash that your shadow is met.

Time reminds me of what I haven't accomplished,

what I want to do,
where I want to be.
It's a tick in my ear and it's irritating.
I scratch to appease it,
but I can't get rid of it.
I need it as much as I despise it.
It's there,
and
it reminds me
it pushes me
it fuels my motivation.

The funny thing is if I make it,
I'm not sure what I'll do.
I wonder what happens after you've done that?
I don't know anyone who has.
People stand on the ledge of greatness,
that's all I know for now.
None of us should dare to look back.

Departure Time: 10:26 p.m.
Arrival Time: Unknown

The motor ran with the ease of a purr, bouncing from the white
strip on the right to its mirroring yellow-double-no
-wait-dashed-no-wait-solid-again line on the left.
The strips formed the only guidance for the vehicle as it moved
through the transparent film of air.
Images were instantaneous, leaving the driver to remember the
moments rapidly, but the reel never ended.
He kept track of the glimpses:
they reminded him of where he came from.
They were a hint to where he would go next,
but there was never a guarantee.
He wished he could see every moment,
but the truck's lights were stronger near their base
and became weaker towards the side.
This caused him to miss some things.
He wanted to experience more.
This insatiable desire angered him.

Was he settling?

The journey's ambivalence
was the reality of the driver's life.
He controlled the vehicle's movements through his views,
but periodically he moved outside the lines, lost track, planned
his detour only to be disrupted
by a roadblock.
The eyes of others looked at him,
blinding him sporadically.
The red, yellow, green intermediates
he had no control over.
At times he was entirely red,
to wonder what was next,
then green again,
the accelerator pressed down.
The orange orbs in the sky
were connected, forming low-hanging smiles.
The silhouettes of the forest's arms
and fingers pointed upward.

The haziness should have deterred him from his goal;
the unexpected, unknown, should have incited insecurity,
but it didn't.
The limbs inspired the driver.
He thought to
follow the lines
stay in between
stay in between
stop at the road
follow the directions.

The fork in the road neared.
He couldn't see it,
but he knew it would be there.
It had been there before,
and sometimes the haze had interrupted his decision.

At times he wished
he could turn and go the opposite way.

This time, at the fork, the lines pointed left.
It was the correct way.
there would be limited obstacles... and... it was safe.

The driver turned right.

The lights, the lines, the directions were gone,
but in the end
he made it home.

I don't care about vanity
as long as people say I'm good looking.

Check-Out

I'm juggling tuna fish cans:
it's the only thing I can afford.
I don't even buy mayonnaise anymore.
Why do I do this?
Well, I'd rather buy another can of tuna fish.

The stack is high and I'm balancing it
against my chest.
I even use my chin as a vise.

This town can't break me.

I know I'll make it,
I know that this is only temporary.
I won't let anything get me down.

The checkout is around the corner
and it's clear – wait...
Damn it.
"Go ahead." I say to the old lady.
The blue cart matches the blue streaks in her hair.
Kitty litter, milk,
and a loaf of white bread.

I think, "Come on – I gotta get going."
"Yes, the milk is $2.39."
"No, there is no sale on the kitty litter."
"Exact change? Are those pennies?"
"She doesn't have enough for the bread?
 You can't be serious!"

I place the cans down
and the belt pulls them closer to the clerk.
I look at the bread.
They both look at the bread.

Vacant stares solve nothing.

The clerk picks it up
and prepares to pass it along to the stock boy.
I stop her.

I look at the old lady's green eyes,
her lids narrow with content.

I pick up one of the cans and
hand it to the clerk.
"Trade ya'?"
I hand her two dollars.
The bread is placed in a paper bag
atop the kitty litter.
The old lady hugs me.
She exits.

I look back to the smaller stack of cans.
Check-out.

She Doesn't Know

The red lipstick
a Longchamp bag
a navy blue Barbour jacket
a wrapped wine bottle (most likely Pinot Grigio)
a box of Godiva chocolates
and fear.

She wonders, "Am I good enough?"

Does she fit the part?
She walks to her seat with a look of confusion.
She wonders about her decisions.
Has she made the right one?

She'd be fine without the labels.
She'd be perfect without anything.
Her mask makes it hard to tell,
but
she doesn't know it.

She's worn it for too long.

The Creation And The Creator

The creator must be alone.
He must sit in the shadows
working on his craft,
a craft that only he was created to do.

The job, distractions, women and men
may not understand the creator.
They can't,
for he is dedicated to his creation.

Careful.

Don't forget your craft.
Hold onto it,
don't let the non-creators steal it
don't let them abuse it
don't let them change it.

Don't let them spoil it.

That would be the worst.
Please, I beg you!
Of all things,
don't let them spoil it.

The creation is the only voice the creator has.
He only speaks when he is ready.
The creator is patient with himself.
The creator is patient with the non-creators.

It's quiet now.
Quiet
Quiet
Quiet
Always quiet.
Is it time to be heard?
Quiet, you!
Is it time to speak?

Quiet, you!
The creator needs it to be quiet.

The creator must be careful.
The creator must believe in his creation.
His creation is not an item for sale.
His creation is intended to inspire.
It's intended to connect the non-creators.

The creation has intention.

Noise starts,
the volume exceeds capacity.
The sparks are shouting.
The creation is ready.
The creator must be alone.

Say something important.

Love Poem To Linda

My heart beats a second beat.
The knowledge of you is painful.
How can I defeat this feeling,
an emotional pull that has no way to succeed?

Love is an instance
a drive
a force that cannot be explained.
For you, it means the world
and you are
my sacrifice
my emotion
my strength.

You're an eternal escape from the ordinary.

For true love is something not defined;
It is a feeling of euphoria.
When a heart flutters and a soul flies:
a sense of what will be and what will become,
the moment of essential peace,
where all substance becomes trivial.

Awake, And A Racing Mind

It seems to always be accompanied by a light
that should be turned off.
A clock
that reads the hours of 3, 4 or 5 a.m.
Eyes
that are caked closed by yellowish-green gook.
My contacts know how to steal moisture.

I try to persuade myself I'm dreaming
or that I need to just lie down again.
But I know my eyes will forgive me
if I take out the contact lenses.
So, I stumble to the bathroom
and squeeze out the fake eyes.
On the return, I stop for a snack,
"What the hell," I say.
I'm up and awake already.
It's quiet then.
I sit at the keyboard and it comes roaring in.
I try to subdue the rapturous calamity of thoughts
sounds
words.

Always words, they're the only thing we've got.

Trying to compartmentalize my thoughts is superfluous.
No one can track the speed at which the mind works.
There are so many words I want to write down,
so many things I want to say to people.

Dispelled,
everything hurls itself at me at this moment.
I can see it,
like a crisp shirt put on for the first time.
Then gone.
A single wear and memory wrinkled.

Trying to pick up the pieces,
any pieces,
to write them down
to spark something later.
Slowly, all gone,
a personal demise
a spit to the eye
a knot in your ear too deep to reach
a stomach drop that trips you to the floor.

The cursor on the screen doesn't move.
I lie down in bed.
Maybe I'll wake up again.
Maybe I'll catch some of the magic.

Let It Shine

Life calls for drama.
Why should it?
We shouldn't have to bear so much pain.
I know how you feel.
You're trying to have a positive outlook,
but it's hard to blind yourself to despair.

All you can do is try to get through it.

It's important to laugh.
Just laugh,
curve your lips into a smile.
Even if tears fall,
even when it seems to be worthless to do so.
Hell, laugh at your misery.
Let it happen.

Let yourself smile.

There's so much pressure in the game of life,
most of which we have no control over,
most of which we are manipulated into feeling.
We're prone to falter,
even if we have trained ourselves to rely on restraint.

Let yourself escape,
escape the world
escape your life for a moment.
There's nothing wrong with stepping away.
Play your favorite song and
close your eyes and listen to yourself breathe.

Only when light hits the exact angle
does it reflect back on us.
Most of the time it can be dark.
Wait for your moment.
When it comes,
let it shine.

Let it shine.

I would rather walk forever than run a marathon.

Write

Write

Write until you can't any more.
Write until you've discovered the magic.
Write until you cry.

Write

Write to inspire.
Write to forgive.
Write to remember.

Write

Write until the greatest story is told.
Write so that you change the world.
Write to touch someone's life.

Write

Write with your heart.
Write for your soul.
Write and never stop.

Write

My Neighborhood's Street

It's 3 a.m., and I'm pedaling against the pavement.
I'll hardly remember this tomorrow.
My street sure will:
it seems to know me well.
It helps guide me to get to my bed.

It's easier to talk to my street.
It is the best listener, and there's little back-talk.
I'm relieved by how it never judges me,
no matter how many times I walk out on it.

Living in a Yesterday Memory

I was waiting for my food.
The room was filling up.
Poppop was eating cinnamon toast.
Meme was finishing an English muffin.

I started to get agitated.
I looked around and saw all the people we knew.
Well, all the people Meme and I remembered.

"Come on, Sue, where's my food?" I asked.
"Sorry, Joe, it's just a little backed up." My sister said.
"But I ordered 20 minutes ago."

"Joe Lee, just be patient." My grandmother,
Meme Marge, said.
"Hey Margey, give the guy a break he's got a big game later
tonight." Poppop said as he winked at me.
I hadn't seen my grandfather give one of those
for a long time.

"Joe Lee... basketball?! He is almost 30 years old,
Poppop - he doesn't play basketball anymore."
"What are you talking about?" I interrupted.
I gave her a look that told her that
it didn't really matter.
"Yeah, Marge, what are you talking about?" Poppop asked.

Meme stopped.
She understood: the reality wasn't worth revealing.
I liked living in Poppop's past.
In it, we were allowed to remember.

These moments were nice.
They were important,
but they were also very sad.
We didn't allow ourselves to be sad.

We dreamed for memories.

I could see Meme struggled.
I suspect it was hard for her to stay strong,
but she did - she had too.
We all had too.

It surprises me how much of a gift reminiscing is.
Conversations you've had - the ones you used to get bored of can
be so precious.

My sister handed me a plate, "Here you go."
"Thanks, Sue."
Poppop looked at Sue and then me.
He was silent.
Meme looked to the side - she couldn't bear witness to it.
I looked at Poppop and he didn't recognize me.
The moment was over
and we didn't know
if another one would ever come.

I felt guilty for forgetting
how valuable memory can be.
I wanted to say that,
but instead I ate the breakfast sandwich.
With each bite I anticipated,
hopeful that Poppop would return.
I waited, only getting four bites
before I couldn't eat anymore.

Sue asked, "Why aren't you eating?"
I didn't say anything.
I started to step away, but stopped.
Poppop said, "Yeah, Joe, you'll need your strength
for the big game today."

*Magic moments are quiet reminders
that madness is soon to follow.*

Mirror Images

I guess we all have an image of ourselves,
and we spend countless hours trying to depict it.
We spend
money
time
and energy to appear to be something we envision.
All so that at one point
at one time
we can be admired as an image.

Although we have ambitions to be original,
we can't be.
Originality is no longer original.
Originality is nothing more
than a false aspiration
and its ugliness builds from the media's vanity.

But we buy into it.
Hoping that one day we will set ourselves apart from
the crowded heap of image seekers,
those who are lost for words or breathe without the opportunity
for acceptance.

We've grown shorter.
We can only expand by recoiling.

We move in a fog created by our culture's
insecurity
excuses
loneliness
delusions
complacency.

October Sidewalks

It starts with socks.
The carefree summer wind that puffed against
my exposed feet are gone.
Socks protect my toes from Fall's burr.
The streets seem wider now.
The nebulous conversations of tourists, interns and visitors have
been taken to their distant homes.
Madison Avenue is full of seekers.
It's the only thing that protects the city.
The loyal veterans mix with the newbies.
Who will persevere?
An unspoken fear presents itself.
Will someone, anyone, make it before you?
Apprehension and hope coincide like oil and water.
Any given day you may be dehydrated.
That's the chance you take.
I walk past Hassan, the kebab cart man.
He hasn't said hello to me all summer,
but it's different today.
Yes, just like every October,
a small sense of trust re-establishes itself,
for those that have survived.
It's the micro-ecosystem,
a city of turbulent transition,
of apathy gone and seasonal ambition
waiting to be fulfilled.
I've made it another year, but hey, look at the time.
I'm late, but aren't we all a little late?

Begin Without Direction

Just start.
Who knows where you'll end up?
Who knows if you'll finish?

Maybe you won't.
That doesn't matter.
Many have ended in places they didn't expect.
Sometimes those places are better,
other times, worse.

But it's better to get somewhere.

Anywhere is better
than no place at all.

Critics and enemies typically drink together.
They have plenty of things in common.

Pragmatism With Love And Women

I can't do this anymore.
It doesn't matter how much I want too.
It doesn't matter how much you want too.

Fuck – Shit – Damn It!

I'm sad,
not because I met you
not because being with you was amazing
not because it can't work
not because I can't speak to you as freely as I used to
not because it will no longer be current.
But because...

You can't fake love.

It was a privilege,
and I know that the severity of everything
makes it hard to believe that.
My words were once the ignition.
Now, I can't even get things started.
There's a pain to all of this,
but it's not the same for me as it is for you.
For me, the pain is knowing
that I will have to try this all again.
The fear, it lingers like an oil drop in water.
It laughs with imbalance,
exposed, trapped and pathetic.

There is nothing to say but goodbye.
With each goodbye, there is a moment that lingers,
a pause
a hope
but the reality is bleak.
Take me back – please – but I can't live!
Why?
Why?
One more try?

I consider it. We consider helping each other.
Can you be the one to alleviate all the pain?

Questions...
Questions upon more questions...
Questions that question every question,
until the heap is tall and the answer is far away.

The tears are not worth it.
We should save them for something more important.
This is no longer it.

This is no longer relevant.

Light a match but don't pull me into it.
There is nothing to consider; the flame will be gone soon.

It's stupid
frustrating
annoying
confusing
despicable
and worst of all, regretful

It's pragmatic, and I hate it
It's the end
It's gone
It's all gone

The Outside People

I can't have a cup of coffee and meet anyone.
Something fresh doesn't seem possible anymore.
I wish I could.
I wish it were like it was years ago,
when seeming cool wasn't cool,
when people really gave a damn
about what they thought,
when they didn't try to mimic something or someone.
Maybe I'm being facetious.
Maybe I don't trust anyone.

I want to believe in people.

We all want too,
but these are such vain times.
Incoherently doomed to feeble success.
The light shines, but it can be too bright.
I look out for the people.
The outside people, that's what I call them.
I take breaks from writing and look out as they walk by.
I want to speak with them.
I want to learn about them.
Why?
To explore,
to beat out the restlessness,
the safety
the security.
Maybe I can learn something from them.
Maybe they can learn something from me.
Maybe it's a waste of time.
Perhaps...
But it would be less asinine
than waiting for them to speak to me.

Fire Breathers

I've been asked why I write poetry,
accused at times of doing it for attention,
to fill the void during parties
to add a topic to a dinner conversation.
It has nothing to do with that:
no,
I do it for myself.
I do it to circumvent therapy:
I don't agree with paying for advice.

But,
besides that,
I keep writing.
I write for the moments when I can't catch a break,
for the searing sense of life's reality that
blurs my vision,
for the riptide of fear, disgust
and revelation that takes me over,
for the comforting clouds that, when opened up,
rain on me with laughter,
for when stomps pinch the ends of my fingers,
for ledges with no abyss,
for flat lined slopes that won't let me trip,
for knives that bend when thrust,
for drinks that affect me like water,
for nerves that shake me steady.

For all of those moments,
I am thankful for poetry.

There's more:
poetry keeps me
from hurting someone else
from corrupting someone else
from falling in love with cynicism.

It allows me
to be alone

to give myself something to believe in
to have temporary relief
to be soothed
to be calm
to give me another day
to force me to believe in tomorrow
to ease the frustration of restlessness
to be me
to think abnormally in a mad world
where I'll be told to be normal.
to say fuck off to conformity,
the establishment and my past,
to be the rebel
to be the introvert
to be the acting extrovert
to scream silently
to get this out
to be selfish
to fill the void that needs attention.

I owe all of this to poetry.

I do it for others as well,
for those that need it,
for those that can't write,
for those that feel low,
for those seeking to speak,
for those looking at clocks wishing they'd move faster.

We've all been there.
Most times I write poetry to avoid feeling that way again.

We all make it through the fire,
and the burns are not as permanent
as others told us they'd be.

My regrets remain my life's realist moments.

Shooting Into Shadows

We're only as good as yesterday.
I know you're questioning your worth.
You're wondering,
"Does it get any better?
Will any moment be better than those past moments?
Is now the best it will ever be?"

If you look back, you'll be shooting into shadows
that glean your insecurities,
but you'll find out,
no matter how hard you try to capture the past,
you can't.
That time was dedicated to that moment,
that memory
that feeling.
And -
It can never be recreated.

The shadows don't intend to create
a bleak sense of your future.
No matter how hard you try to hold onto
the spirit, the innocence and the love for yesterday,
the harshness of reality
soundly loses to youth.

It's your choice how you endure the present.
You can stay back, but the past is always familiar.
Or you can move forward
and never look back into the shadows.

Looking forward, your life will get better.
New doors
new people
new experiences
new moments
will unveil themselves.

That is the truest beauty in life,
and you can't find it
unless you can.
Remember,
but never try to recreate.

Your time is short.
Don't blow it.
There is so much light for you.
There is so much more for you.
Today is much brighter than yesterday,
and tomorrow is even brighter.
Never look back, never.
A life in darkness is easy,
but it's a life wasted by regret.
Never recreate regret.
Never swallow in the sorrows.
Never shoot into the shadows.

Bohemian

I'm living now,
and I'm living in the past.
Some things change gradually.
There's advancement,
 - sure, even corruption -
but it's all the same in the end.
The visions
The access
Everything will appear to be at your fingertips,
but that's just the scene.
A deliberate machination,
a plan to distract us from thinking freely.

A clouded mind is produced entirely
by our faults.

It's easier to not speak than to be heard,
but at the very least, listen.
Follow a path that calls to you.
Resist questioning for the pure sake of questioning.
Find yourself and differentiate.
Avoid following the herd.

Be a rebel.

But even rebels form communities,
don't they?
I'm just not sure what to believe in.
Should I just remain thinking on my own?
I'm not sure of anything.

That's common ground for everyone.
Does our decision affect only us in the end?
Maybe not.

Does this have to be so complicated?
Most like to make it harder than it needs to be,
because without struggle there is no satisfaction.
Compliments always feel forced.
I don't know how to respond to them
when I know they aren't deserved.
I don't know how to act.
I don't know,
and I hope I never learn.

As It Echoes

I thought I'd be farther along by now.
The pixels are gnats eating away at my brain.
It's only Thursday and I'm already thinking
about when the biweekly will clear.
Bills drive me.
A prisoner to the desk.
9 hours.
A meager meal at noon.
Tomorrow, it'll be just as glamorous.

A generation promised to succeed.

Every aspect of my life set by thirty.
I'm 28 and I need an extension.
I don't know what's going to happen.
It's not like I have any control anyhow,
and that's the way it's supposed to be.
I shouldn't wait:
it's the universal sign of politeness,
waiting to write,
waiting to leave my job,
waiting more than two months for her to come around.

But I wait - just like everyone else.

Call it whining,
but ambition and passion shouldn't be held back.
The right people don't win.
You have to know somebody to get in with somebody.
Who needs a connection anyway?
Dang, I don't need a connection.
Well, I guess I need a connection.
Where do you get a friggin' connection?
Fuck, I can't do this without a connection!!!
What's worse is knowing you can do something,
but are forced to compromise
it's worth.

Fuckin' Ey!
Why can't I get an agent?
Why can't I get a script sold?
Why can't anybody read my stuff?
Hell, I'd rather take a call telling me
how awful I am, then wait this long.

Resentment creates a piece of clothing
stitched with a fine thread of passive aggression.

We are trained not to say anything.
Paralyzed by the pedigree of society's injustice.
Waiting, hopeful, delusional:
they all encapsulate our state of mind.
There are the lucky ones,
the ones that break out
or at least appear to.
I know some of them.

They are the most quiet.

Turned into puppets, they watch us.
Sometimes they cry out in the night.
They act like it's someone else.
I hear it as it echoes.
I know it's them.
Then, we're together.

Through the echoes of longing.
Through the echoes of success.

The voices are heard by those that want to hear them.
I know my voice will be heard.
Maybe I'll make it?
What else is there to do?

*Far more people like to portray being creative
than actually creating anything at all.*

If You Give Me A Gold Star I'll Take A Shit On It

Please don't tell me I'm great.
Don't tell me I'm doing well.
No, don't say anything to me.
Exclude me from your conversations.
Set me aside.

But when you need to beat someone,
use me as your punching bag.
No, don't include me in the dinners.
No, don't ask me about my family.
No, don't talk to me at all.
Why would you?
I don't fucking matter.

That's where you're wrong.
I shouldn't be scared of you.
Your power is weak.
Silence is your only weapon,
but I've come to know that.

It's the only thing you've got,
and as much as you think it hurts me, it doesn't.
I laugh at you when you're not around.
I want to make fun of how scared you are!
You're an idiot!

I feel sorry for you:
stuck,
hoping that I'll come around,
wishing I was near.
Who else do you have?
I have plenty, I have others that don't place me aside.

I have more than you.

You may have more than me,
but that doesn't matter.
I'm full where it matters.
I have my own beat,
and it has nothing to do with you.

From a Text I Don't Remember

The journey is a vast, arduous one.
An impressionable cave.
Full of
fear
assumptions
feelings of inferiority.

It takes a strong-willed person,
to make it.

Fear is something we don't understand;
it's something realized by vulnerable souls.

Dashboard Debris
(Childhood Joyrides)

The empty packs of cigarettes
were always in high demand,
Newport layered atop Marlboro.
Luxury lasted as long as the thrill
that comes on the first of the month.
The State check goes in a week,
Lisbon knew how to live with joyous brevity.

To the right,
more towards the middle,
just off to the right of the steering wheel
was an Uncle Henry's,
the precursor to craigslist.
Online, you would click and email,
in the pamphlet,
you would crease pages and call later.

We'd go to Big Apples every week.
The gas was a little cheaper there.
The ads hit the newsstand on Tuesdays.

"Hell, look here, that's a deal!"
He'd say that at least ten times thereafter.
I don't think we ever made a deal while in Lisbon.

Deals never seemed to come to fruition.

It was always exciting to think one could.

On the passenger's side, the side that I used to call,
"my side,"
The fast food bags and loose dried-out French fries mingled with
pencils
pens
chewed Green Mountain coffee cup lids
crushed Moxie soda cans
and tapestries of Slim Jim beef jerky wrappers.

The tangle always looked exactly the same.
In spring and summer I'd roll down the window and let pieces
fly out.
Sometimes I couldn't bear it.
This happened less often in the winter,
when I wouldn't dare roll down my window.

If it ever got too thick,
when it was too difficult to see the road ahead,
I'd clean it.
He would never say thank you.
I didn't need it.
He knew I appreciated the ride.

We're all imposters,
scammers
and crooks.

The key is getting away with it.

There's a Thin Line Between Happiness and Struggle, and You Tend to Lean Towards Struggle

Are you happy?

No, wait, don't answer so quickly.
Don't say yes, no, or anything else.
Just think about it.
Think about when you wake up.
Think about the people in your life.
Think now - just think.

Don't think about someone else.
Don't think about what they have.
Don't think about what you have.
Don't think about what you don't have.
Don't think with you head.
Don't...

Think with your heart.
Think with your soul.
Think about today.
Think about tomorrow.

Think about being happy.

Tacos with Guacamole

She stood behind me,
just as distant as if she weren't there at all,
convincing herself that there wasn't,
and never would be,
anything between us.
And, for the first time in a long time,
I was okay with that.
I didn't need to hope
or suspect that something would happen.

I was okay.

Did I want it to be over?
Did I think I should let it go?
No, that was never my nature.
So, while we waited for the fish tacos,
I felt some pressure on my back.

She leaned on me.

It wasn't anything out of the ordinary.
It wasn't anything different
than another friend leaning on another friend.

It wasn't anything at all,

until I felt it was everything.
She'll never know that.
Well, that's what I think for now.
I wish it were different sometimes.

Vulnerability squanders a man's strength.

It doesn't matter; it's best to be stunted.
I guess feelings are worse for those who have them.
But I'll be okay.
I'll take her lean.
We'll both live the fantasy for the moment.

That's all I need... for now.

I wonder what she needs.

Maybe that's my biggest drive.
Maybe it's no one right now.
I hope one day it might be me.
That's selfish,
it really is,
because you can't wait on someone:
It doesn't work that way,
It never does and it never will.

Finding a connection is rare these days.

To force one is false,
to imagine one is eternal,
to experience one is everything.
I don't know what'll happen with us.
So I'll take tonight,
I'll take what she gives me.

Her Pages

She doesn't open up to anyone.
There's a story she intends to tell,
a way she wants to be remembered.

Once, I wrote on Her pages.

There was a certain
time
moment
feel,
a style that worked.
I filled each page.
I wrote carefully.
She watched carefully.
I tried diligently to pacify Her.

All I wanted to do was create a love story.

At first, it was easy,
then it got harder.
I didn't even want to look at Her pages.
I feigned writer's block.
I didn't want to write about what hurt:
those times
of drunken spats
of jealously
of presumption
of fear.

Our relationship crumbled over nothing.

I would get so mad at her.
She in turn was just as caustic.
But after times of retaliation and disgust,
we'd turn Her pages.
Completely blank, white.
We'd come together.
We wouldn't say anything.

We realized how foolish we were,
how it didn't matter,
how it 'happened' in the last chapter.

I shouldn't,
but I can't help remembering.

It is always the small things I miss the most,

the midnight hair,
the gap in between the top middle teeth,
the dot under the right eye,
the chunky, button nose,
the curve along her back.
Those were hers.

I'm sure there were things about me
that must be
noted in Her pages.
I never was able to read those.
I'll never get the chance.

Our days were numbered.
Pages thinned
until the last one came,
when the story had to end.
It was so good.
I was selfish; maybe I still am.
I wanted to know more.
I wanted to write more.
I wanted to read more.
I wanted Her more.
But she didn't,
she didn't want me anymore.

So I wrote.
I couldn't procrastinate any longer.
It took me longer to write "The End"
than any word before it.

After I finished, she took Her pages.
I needn't write about them ever again.

Sometimes I try to remember,
senselessly trying to figure out
what part might I have changed to make it work.
I could rattle my mind around it forever, I suppose.
Perhaps I should find someone new.

Any guy is lucky to write in Her pages.

They just don't know how much
until they notice the pages thinning.
When it's almost time to write:
"The End"

I can't sing you a song,
but I can write something
that'll inspire you to write one.

Pushing

Why do I push people?
Why?
When I'm just about to let them in,
just when I think I can,
I push
I push one last push.

I want to know how far I can take it.
It's a test I use to see how loyal people are.

I'm pushing myself when I do this.
Maybe it's wrong of me,
maybe it seems cruel,
but if I let them betray me,
I'll be the fool.
I'll get pushed to the side with the others,
and be left wallowing in the misery of
cruelty
deceit
lies
and loneliness.

I can't allow myself to feel that way.
So I push.
I push.
I push!

Is there someone strong enough to push me back?

I know if they can take it,
they will be there for me.
In turn,
I'll be there for them.

I can't wait until I don't have to push anymore.

Therein lies the trouble.
Everyone's pushing.
Everyone
If only we could stop
lying
cheating
vendettas.

Then we could stop.
Then we could stop
pushing.

Fight Nights

I just need a reason.
Really, anything will do.
There's tension right now.
I'm waiting for any moment.
Beer five stares back at me.
It lubricates my intentions.
I just want to fight.
Yeah, that's right – fight!
I know I have a good job.
I know I have a good family.
Yes, I know this is a stupid decision.
I want it.
I need it.
It's not the booze that's causing this.
Well, maybe it convinces me slightly.
It's not the reason though.
It's about me feeling like I have to have something.
A voice?
I guess.
A say?
Yes, absolutely.
My anger flames inside me.
The tranquility of a cool summer's eve belies my rage.
If only my fire wouldn't burn so deep.
No one deals with this except me.
I'm ready for it,
a flinch
a look
anything.
Even abnormal breathing would set me off.
I want it, but I don't know why.
That's when I stop.
I just look at the beer.
It's almost empty.
One more?
No,
five is my limit.
The bartender shoos me away.

I've won.
Only I know it.
The door is the last thing I remember.
A victory lap awaits me outside.
I'm led forward by Broadway.
The streets always direct me home.
Tomorrow, I'll come back.
The drinks will be served,
the bar will be waiting,
and the fight will rise.
I'll be ready,
I'll stop it before it gets too far.

The buildup is enough.
Sometimes enough is worth it all in the end.

The Crowd's Beauty

There's beauty inside all of us.

We mustn't let it go.
When you test your beauty with others, be careful.
You'll be called different.
You'll be called abnormal.
You'll be called many things
that come from someone else's envy.
They'll wonder if your beauty makes theirs ugly.
Don't listen to their questions.

Never forget how precious your beauty is.

Something happened to them along the way.
They've forgotten and wish they could be pure.
So they'll challenge you.
You'll wonder if you should be like them.
Possibly, they're right.
Maybe you should refuse your beauty.
Don't: that's exactly what they want.

Only you need to celebrate your beauty.

It doesn't matter how much others applaud.
A crowd of claps follows.
It takes strength to remain silent.
So learn about your beauty.
Make it better with each day.

Even if you are the only one to see it.

The stars receive their glow
from the crazy diamonds shining below.

Belmont

I look to the starting gate, but it's too far to see.
I don't mind: the real action is below me.
I'm glad to be in the rafters.
The beasts are awaiting for the release of their prey.

Pockets of species sit in the lower grandstand.
Men with growing guts smoking cigars
as rapidly as pencil-thin women puff Virginia Slims.
Women hide their wallows in fragile peacock-like hats.
College kids swim in a golden sea of amnesia.
Children, who remain the purest species,
fantasize about becoming jockeys.

And they're off!
The fire of the gun stuns us.
There's a moment of complete silence.
Everyone is a part of this moment.
The start.
Afterwards, everyone is on their own.

"Come on Wicked Strong!"
"Come on Medal Count!"
"Come on Commissioner!"
"Come on California Chrome!"

I root for California Chrome.
He won't make me a fortune.
The odds are terrible,
but I want to be a part of history!

We all hold our white betting slips like lottery tickets.
The only difference is that everyone
has a chance the entire way.

Down the home stretch and everyone rises,
beers spill,
once-prized hot dogs and nachos splat.
Everyone forgets reality
for two minutes and thirty seconds.

After the horses cross the finish line,
it start snowing.
In the midst of a mid-summer evening,
each snowflake -
"Belmont, race ten, two dollars to win on the five"
once holding some value -
"Belmont, race ten, fifty dollars to show on the three"
once holding some hope -
"Belmont, race ten, twenty-three dollars to place on seven"
each snowflake -
lasting for two minutes and thirty seconds.

It's Closer Than You Think

It's getting crowded.
The bumps come more frequently,
until we have no choice
but to scatter chaotically.
As if we were exploding fireworks.
Soon we fall,
the sparks run dry.
Crowded, again, we seek to find our purpose.

Where is your life going to take you?

Numerous clouds grow, and
each hovers with unfulfilled ambivalence.
Resilient to rain, everything stays dry.
It's colder, and that's becoming normal.
It was like this yesterday, and tomorrow will be the same.

Time should not just pass.

I can see why people regret getting out of bed.
It'd be easier to sleep the day away.
They wouldn't have to hear the noise,
the letdown that comes from
unfulfilled purpose
superfluous emails
power trips
inferior minds.
They wouldn't have to call this "life."

And you deserve to define yourself.

Obstacles,
from the outsiders, from the insiders, from yourself
will always try to deter you.
Run from these restraints.
Hell, run away from everything.
The pace of accomplishment is grueling.
Never quit.

Sometimes we don't know when we'll finish a race.
Sometimes we don't even know how to start.

There'll be a rearview mirror in front of us.
It asks us to keep up going,
just a little longer.
It tells us to hold on.
That's the hardest part of it all.

Remember to always pursue your dream.

It's a bitch of a decision if you don't.
Forgetting seems to happen
when glancing at the mirror
becomes too tiring.

Only weak individuals resist looking at their reflection.

Change comes if you wait.
Flashes of light catch us in unexpected moments.
They remind us,
no,
dare us to keep moving.

We have to fight to attain personal glory.

Remember to believe.
Even when the odds are against you.
Even when you're weary about the present.
Even when the mirror seems too far away.
Run, run to it.

Everything you ever wanted is closer than you think.

Genius

A word used too frequently,
sprayed into our faces like confetti,
each scrap of color lofting,
a convention manifested by social superiority.
A temporary sense of suspended euphoria.

At the party everyone wonders,
why didn't
you
I
or someone else think of that before?

Afterwards, the broom's bristles kiss the confetti,
piles of glorious shrapnel
ready for the garbage,
mixed among the
cups
plates
and moldy cheese platters,
forgotten piles of the evening's grandeur,
until tomorrow,
when everyone celebrates the new burst of genius.

Dream of a place
where all of your anxiety
dwindles away.

I Pretend To Be On This Side

My best side is one I only let few see.
Here, I'm the funny guy.
Sure, I'll be the guy that takes the blame.
I suppose that's my role from 9-5.

I can't show my best side to them.

Why?
Because if I did that
I wouldn't have my job
I couldn't go to the parties.

And for God's sake, I couldn't miss another party!

I hate the fucking parties.
I hate being around fake friends.

I hate pretending to be that side.

Milk Carton

Some people will never know how great they are.
Life can become a tempting trick.
We are victimized by the yearning to emulate
someone or something you see.
Turn off
the computer
the phone
the TV
and close the books.
Don't even read this damn poem!

How rare is it that we think for ourselves?

Walking
is something that we take for granted.
Thinking
has become a strain.

Until we place ourselves in a position
where we hope to be included
where we hope to feel we belong.

No one belongs anywhere.

We are all wanderers,
travelers with no place to go,
transiently moving towards some unknown location,
an existence
based on the belief that at some point we'll make it.

We live in a lost world.

I would say have a safe trip,
but there is nothing safe about anyone's journey.

Withdrawn Burden

(Generation, Millennial)

When I think of Millennials,
I see a generation
victimized by incomprehensible stimulus,
free-flowing thought lost by
the overbearing immensity of information
unleashed by the endless aqueducts of technology,

hobbies enjoyed only for their potential
to become businesses,
the joy of life's experiences hastened by the tantalizing prospect
that profit could be made from it,
life based on the quality of dollars,

relationships full of vanity,
The pride in appearance has become a consistent bore.
The envy of celebrity dispels
the fervor to be different.
The bleeding incongruity of life calls for an audience
to be listened to by a pack of non-thinkers.

Why is no one asking questions?
You ask, what type of questions?
Questions of themselves.
Question to others.
Any questions.
Any.
anything at all.

Superfluous challenges turn capable minds
into inferior gossips
busied by the vapid wildness of distractions,
priority of life taken verbatim,
inspiration sourced from disingenuous accomplishment,
admiration based on "likes" and "views"
instead of letters,
impressions lasting only for a moment.

I fear the term "icon" will perish.
I can't think of a
Hemmingway
Fitzgerald
or even a Bukowski
Living in this day in age.

We give ourselves soft pats on the back
for choosing to get up today.
Sensibility is trumped by cynicism.
Diligence is outweighed by entitlement.

This generation has become withdrawn,
confined to a periscope view of the world,
a narrow vision blinded by the vast possibilities,
binning themselves even before giving
other avenues a chance.
Overwhelmed by it all,
It seems no one is willing to take on the burden.

Memory is a disadvantage
if achievement has yet to be fulfilled,
but the moments before actualization
straddle the fine line between desire and complacency,
both of which glean dichotomous resolutions.
Where will you end up?
It depends how much you want to remember.

#lifestyle

The
year
is
young
and
debauchery
will
ensue.

The Complex

There's a lingering sense of urgency.
It appears to come from anticipation,
possibly stemming from a deep desire to make it.
To do it.
To do something.
To make an impact.

That's why I can be dangerous.

I wouldn't harm anyone,
but that leaves me.
I don't have a safety net.
If I fell there would be nothing to catch me.
So why do I do it?
What's the point in trying to beat the odds?

It's something you're born into.

The ones that have it already have tried to derail me.
Their opposition never comes from my ability.
Only I can make the final decision to stop,
but there's a problem for my opposition:

I don't know how to stop.

My longing allows me to overcome
the quiet vacancy of not knowing if it will happen.
But I wait for it.
I believe.
I know people are there, counting on me.

No one will ever know how much they impact others.

Quitting is something that doesn't define you either.
But, if it is, then you'll give up.
So leave now.
Let the next person take your place.

You won't.
It takes many people to end something.

It takes one person to start it.

The Wild Revolve

I don't even know why sometimes.
There's an impeccable rush,
yet I'm scared I'm going to lose it all the time,
but I thrive on it, live on it and hate it all at once.
Now, here I am babbling about it
and feeling completely normal,
here in a small bar, just like the one in Lewiston.
Everything is easy back there
and I've left it.
I could always go back.
It's my choice, I guess, but – I don't.
I refuse too.

Now I'm beating the bar's counter like a drum.
With each thump, I yell,
"Wild, Wild, Wild."
The bartender looks at me as if this is completely normal.
"Did you know that I lie down with the lights on at night?"
He laughs because I've told this to him ten times before.
I try to calm down,
but a radical image circulates inside my head:
A deranged carousel
out on the west side of Central Park.

As its gears start,
my shortcomings coincide with the beauty of chance.
I can't help myself.

I believe in chance.

My belief allows me to beat inertia's grasp,
and the ride spins, faster and faster, and the wildness of it all
consumes me.
I don't get off, I don't ask the conductor to press stop.
I hold on,
for dear fucking life, I hold on!
It'd be easier to let go.
I never should have gotten on this ride.
But when I say that, it isn't me.
It isn't true.
I'm stuck and completely captivated,
addicted to the wild revolve.

Passion comes from those
who don't know any better.

The Work Day

The elevator rings and the doors open to the 9th floor.
I rush to the clock-in station.
It reads my hand.
8:59 a.m.
I just made it.

I'm so lucky to be here.

The computer screens laugh at me all day.
The passive aggressiveness tells me that I'm not in charge.
Emails... no one speaks anymore.
"This is your role, not mine. But I'll take the credit."
"Oh, I said to do that – well I changed my mind – do this."
"Why hasn't this been done yet? – don't delay."

I'm so lucky to be here.

Thanks for treating me like shit.
But I'll play the part.
I'll smile a plastic smile.
I'll agree with whatever you say.
You won't know the difference.

I'm so lucky to be here.

I need the money.
I need it for the pit I live in.
I need to keep the rats company
as they run through my walls while I try to sleep.
I need to feed the dog that shits and pisses
next to my bed.
I need to hear the walls slam
as my roommate pleases a woman.

I'm so lucky to be here.

It's quiet after 4 p.m.
I take the last hour to eat lunch.
There was no time before.
Busy, Busy, Busy – being busy.
It's all noise – but the show must go on!
A distraction from what I really want to do.

I'm so lucky to be here.

I look forward to later.
I'll sit down and write.
Yes, sit down and write.
Here is where I remember.

I'm so lucky to be here.

Light Sleeper

I fell asleep in my room with all the lights on.
I know that it will happen again.
My life is moving so quickly this year,
illuminated by a fresh drive.

I feel so alive.

Anyone can hide behind darkness.
But I don't want to hide.
Not like I did last year.
No, I only want to be in the light.

Momentum With Her

My bed's vacancy was unusual.
The refrigerator's hum became a consistent voice for me.
It let me know I was still alive.
The dashing cars sprinted through the puddles.
The rain had left hours ago,
and so too had its soothing sound.
I yearned for one last drop.

The window's shades were razor blades.
Light ate through.
I had yet to hang curtains.
The beams shone on my floor and
reminded me of a concert I had attended.
No one was performing now.
I was the only one in the crowd.
I sat,
I thought about everything I could do.
All of the people I could be with,
but I didn't move.

I remained, thinking of her.

The anticipation of a Saturday evening
is a cultural fallacy.
The curt pleasantries meander.
The preliminary intoxication sets a dreary tone.
The bars wait,
it calls.
In some cases it beckons with a yell.
The verve for
acceptance
meaning
or any sort of feeling
waits at the base of a glass laced with foam and amber.
Another round?
Fill it up!
I'm still trying to find it!
I'm yelling now,
I'm mad for it.
Just like everyone else.

Later,
there is nothing.
I envy myself in those times.
The ability to be so free.
I'm no longer anxious.
It won't be long before I will be again.
There's nothing to hold the listless nature of inebriation.
I've lost the ability to care when I most need it,
and it is because of those times.
I know
the sound of loneliness is better than hearing nothing at all.

I'm unsure,
but
I think of her.
Is she the answer?
I don't know.

Without her I don't think I can find an answer.

In turn she looks for something.
Is it the same as me?
Maybe?
Most likely not.
It's hers alone.
So we learn to grow together.
Remind each other that together,
we are better.

Anyone can hear you,
but that's not being there.

It was inevitable I guess.
Maybe it isn't even up to me.
Being alone takes its toll,
Though not always so clearly at first
It allows you to think
It makes you stop
It makes you understand
Stopping momentum is difficult.

It typically occurs when least expected,
In times when you completely crash.
Be angry?
Why?
It won't persist;
You'll speed up again,
Tuned up for the next ride.

Light from a car streams through the shade again.
It's moving differently now.
The puddles are grazed not shattered.
I still hear the hum of the refrigerator.
When I look to my bed,
Still
She is not there
She used to be
Always
But now it's calling her again,
and I know the next time the cars drive by and the light cuts the
floor
I won't hear the hum after
I hear a voice.

She'll always be my sweet baby.

I want to remain
wild,
naïve
and delusional;
at least then,
dreams remain tangible.

Drift With the Others or Move the Cursor

The parties
The job
The booze
The ridiculous family expectations.

The thought killers.

Washed away like driftwood in the sea.
Further and further it goes,
heading for the infinity of sky and sea.

Poisoned by the killers.

A man needs to be alone.
It can be the most frightening experience,
but if he allows for it to happen,
he'll understand himself more.

The killers don't understand themselves.

Don't answer the calls,
the texts,
the goddamn snapchats.
Technology has only served to disrupt your thinking.
Yes - it's important.
Yes - it's turned out to be essential.
But if you're caught flipping through a clear screen,
the cursor waiting to write the story of your life will blink
blink
blink.

Don't wait on the killers.

They won't ask about your real thoughts.
Don't wait to say something great.
Only you need to listen.
Say something important.

Your thoughts are salvageable.
They're yours to present to the stupid world.
No one can re-create your manifestations.
The killers can try and copy,
yes, the killers can steal and try to pretend to be others.

In the end your thoughts don't belong to the killers.

Once you believe that,
the cowards that
tweet,
text
and yearn for 'likes' will drift away without you.
They'll try to swim upstream.

The killers will be soon forgotten.

You'll be alone.
The sun will be in your face.
Your hair will flicker
as the wind slowly massages each strand.
And you'll think some more.
You'll believe some more.

You'll create some more.

And once you're done,
it'll be waiting for more.
The cursor that is
Blinking
Blink
Blink

Joy Ride

'Cause if you gonna' ride with me,
it's not about getting away.
It's about getting there,
finding what's next,
meeting people,
all types of people,

The stranger the better.

I don't want safe.
I like the border
between crazy and wild,
possessed and insane,
ruthless without being reckless.

That's what I want.

That's who I can relate to.
If you don't want that,
I would suggest stayin' away.
It wouldn't be exactly how you'd want it.
But if that's your game,
join me on this joy ride.

All Roads to Youth End In Austin, Texas

We were preverbal creatures of the night,
sipping on cheap drafts
listening to open mic
and relying on optimism.
A community of drunken Millennials,
the beast of the night tantalizes us.

Our spirits are mesmerized by hope, fear and desperation.

It's better to be here
than anywhere else.

I look out to my former soul,
the one that yearned to feel.

The way youth tricks you into believing.

I watch and can't help it.
I miss that sense of adventure
and the thrill of optimism.

I've come to know the confines of my life are narrowing.

Am I running?
From the person I'm supposed to be?
I'm not sure.
I try to believe there's still time for me to explore.

I need a moment alone to regain composure.

Kelly walks over and asks, "Are you okay, buddy?"
"I am,
I'm not,
I'm not really sure," I tell her.
I know that I envy the times when I felt lost,
The times when my spirit shouted.

I miss hearing the sound of my youth.

The group reminds me
of the dreams I've had
of the dreams that remain.
A quiet desperation follows,
a lifetime journey to reach a moment.

When we gasp our truest breath.

The end of youth is something so fragile.
It escapes us in the moment when we wish for it most.
Society pressures us,
not in the sense of exploring,
but in the urgency of time.
It ticks, rattles and infuriates us.
I wish it were not so,
but I guess it has to be.
Something needs to remind us how ignorant it is to waste.

Time is a callous notice that forever isn't forever.

The night,
a black curtain cast over a gray past.
We yearn to experience everything for the first time.
But instead we grow.
Still, we resist.
At times -
We're desperate to forget.
At other times -

We're desperate to remember.

The pull outweighs the restraint, and we push forward
Even when it's easier not too.
As long as we believe in the rarity of light,
we hold on to that belief
For we know that even the most delusional individuals have
prevailed.

A memory becomes a victim to emotion.

A sense of our present banality laughs at us
while we yearn to repeat the past,
to step into our former selves,
as if born again and experiencing everything
for the first time.
When the thrill of discovery was fresh.
But we're distracted during first experiences.
Unable to fully appreciate them,
we become victims only later.

Ailed by nostalgia.

But the beers keep on coming.
The songs keep on playing.
The misfits and I cheer on another round.
Danny is on stage,
about to pull some chords.
We take it in.

I'm sad now.
Unlike the others,
I've been here before,
and tomorrow comes too quickly.

I'll miss this.

When the trip's over and I return to my daily doldrums,
I'll miss this even more.
And
even in the later days when I'm much older than now,
after many more stories and experiences pass me by,
I'll think back on tonight, think about right now.

I'll miss it.

Success won't kill you, the passion to get there will.

I Don't Resist - I Should - But I Don't

I could write about her.
That's not how it always is with the girls.
The worst part?
Sometimes the ones you write about are no good.
Those girls...they're a bad habit for me.
I can't help it.
I don't stop myself.
I'm more inspired to write about them,
than the other girls.

Penne alla vodka

It's -11 degrees Celsius
and I'm holding a blistering cold tray
of Penne alla vodka.
It was left over from the weekly meeting.
I stayed late so I could secure it.
I couldn't let it go to waste!
Money is tight this month and every bit helps.
I just wish it was not wrapped in tin foil.

I'm rushing – trying to beat my breath in front of me.
Everything is cold.
The bikes are cold.
The trashcans are cold.
The mailbox is cold.
The goddamn penne pasta is cold!

I can't move my fingers,
they are burning – and the tips are on fire.
Rigor mortis sets in and my right hand is stuck.
I'm balancing the tray and shaking the other one.
"Come on hand, stop burning."
This makes absolutely no sense!

I slip on black ice
as I turn the corner of 44th and Broadway.
I drop the pasta.
Its scatters all over the ground.
The sauce hardens like icing on a concrete cake.
The noodles become brittle,
thirsting to soften under hot water.
My right glove remains stuck to the pan.
I rip it off and place it back over my hand.

I walk up the stairs to my apartment.
The moment I enter the mail area,
my hands are revived.
All I can think about is the Penne alla vodka.
Should I go back and get it?
Yes – but no – I can't.
It must be frozen to the ground by now.
The rats will be first to gnaw at it.

I get to my door.
I'm hungry.
I'm exhausted.
Pocket or Jacket?
Where are my keys?
I don't have my friggin' keys!

I will have to go out in the chill again.
I will have to go
on the subway
back to work
and get the goddamn keys off my desk!

But before all of that,
I will have to walk past
the fucking Penne alla vodka...

The UFC Fighters

These are the bravest of souls.
They have to be.
They have to sacrifice everything to win.
Hours don't pass by in the gym.
No, time passes in days, weeks and months.
Sometime the chance
they've been waiting for years to arrive.

Long spats of self-discipline.
Family, friends, husbands and wives become strangers.
They stay hidden within cold gymnasiums.
They spare and condition.
They starve.
They stay focused in a world full of doubt,
but they can never doubt.
The moment they start, they lose forever.

It takes a wild woman or man to stay in this game.
Who in their right mind closes their eyes,
and imagines punches and kicks being thrown at them,
maneuvering in front of mirrors,
while forced,
the entire time,
to look at their biggest opponent...
themselves
wondering, wondering,
are they good enough?
Yes, yes that's why they've become fighters!

They've pushed themselves
to the edge of human insanity.
Boundaries are only steps away,
It'd be so much easier for them to jump.
Just like the rest of us.
But they don't,
they look down and can't bear to be pure mortals.
Their life's purpose has requested more.

The saddest part is, for most,
the purse will always be low.
The purse may disappear completely.
Age has taken too many victims,
and even the best must come to understand
that age ends everything.

For the chosen ones,
the ones that can't accept any of these realities,
the ones that can't think about anything,
can't imagine doing anything else,
the ones that have no fear
the ones willing to die,
the type of individuals we all wish,
just once, to be,
the ones we watch for,
the ones we pray for,
the ones we agonize for,
the ones we cry for,
no matter in victory or defeat,

A life, a fighter
dedicated to the UFC.

Denial is a virtue.

The Opposite Side Of Time

Time,
it's the fucking helicopter on your back.
Hovering over every move.
A goddamn reminder of what you've wanted
and
of how little you have.

I'm always rushing.
Rush
Rush...
Screw you, rush!

I don't prescribe to the, "It was meant to be."
No,
fuck off, man, if you believe that.
I'm going to make it happen.
I'm too goddamn stubborn.
I'm too goddamn ambitious.
I'm too goddamn crazy.

I'm going to get there.
I will!
As for time,
it won't be on my side.

American Chess
(Everyday Dishonest Heroes)

The children will learn about it,
ways they can maneuver,
weave,
and bob.
They'll play on empathy
and use emotion to disguise their inability,
their lives lived as decoys.

In this game of life,
they'll capitalize on the loopholes,
they'll become masters of social deception,
debunking diligence,
discipline,
and dedication,
trained to dismiss
anything that glistens with accountability,
skilled in passive aggression -
liable to nothing -
with nothing made
nothing moved
nothing
nothing at all.

The teachers will teach them this
because the teachers were once them.
The subject matter covered up
a dazzling display of subjective adaptability.
Confused by the teachers,
confused by the parents,
they are taught to be confused
by the ones they admire the most.

We grow up into a society that
bins us
rewards us
labels us.
All too quickly, it finds a way to belittle us,
leaving adults groomed to battle endlessly
against one another.

For, how quickly do we turn
when we aren't given
the applause?
That's when the evil comes out.
The growth of anything is subdued.
The endless desire to be
wanted and regarded,
a misbelief that we need to be placed
in a position of prestige,
a foretelling of the loss of our potential,
that's what we've learned.
And so,
Americans are bred to be withdrawn.

They say mental health will save us all,
but how can we believe the therapist who needs therapy
or prescribes us the drugs to keep us -
needing them
paying them,

the tax dollars of the hardest workers
spent on those who
act,
who've had bad parenting,
who knows manipulation is better than any talent?
They play the finest game.
The country's progress will be stunted by the game.
Fear of omission will ignite its flames.

Everyone will burn from the
intolerable
apprehensible
insanity
of the game.

For those fighting for honor,
lurking alone and creating,
the dice will roll their roll,
the numbers will lie,
and they'll never break the bank.

When the child
weeps
begs
gives us an honest answer,
we dismiss them as being weak.
When the child is
silent
attempts to take his life
where he hides behind a manacle mask of deceit,
we call him brave.
The country gives him money, a home, food, and a therapist.
All the attention
he could ever expect of US.

Honesty is dangerous.
Those who bear truth
become ingenuous victims of the game.
It turns on them.
It eats them up.
It makes them the worker bee,
dismisses the intellect they harbor,
places them far away from
power
innovation
and instead places them under the direction of monsters,
those that ensure advancement falls in on itself,
as if it were a bridge,

built so long,
yet just as the last peg remains
the entire structure collapses,
only to start the project once more.

This is America.
This is the price paid by hardworking individuals.
This is the land of the free.
This is the land of the careless.
We bask in a sad disarray,
chaos mixed with resounding ignorance based on
the delays in
development
possibility
and ambitions.

The government will tell us what they want.
The media will show
whatever someone else pays them to show US.
The people will believe them,
give their lives
to hear what they're told to do.
They will follow like herds of antelope to water.
Seeking nothing more than
the easiest direction
to eat and digest the food
and then crap it out;
then, when hungry again,
seek the next feast.

Movement remains torrid and without direction.
Our intuition struck down.
The spirit of any man ripped out of him
before it has time to commit itself.
The darkest days darkened
by the looming disappointment.
The internal disbelief.
The capturers await their prey,
the prey is already defeated.

Brilliant men turned into store clerks.
Store clerks turned into presidents.
If only the paper were blank from the start,
the teachers would allow us to explore.
If only the goals were cohesive,
then progress could prevail.
If only the game didn't exist,
then, the insanity wouldn't ruin minds.

A shimmering cape waits to be swung over our eyes,
attention taken away
by this distraction -
or that distraction,
with more distraction waiting,
until nothing is clear.
Fog hovers in front of us,
keeping us humble.
And if we dare to look past it,
our eyes will shut,
they'll remain shut,
until we fall complacent again.

It can get you down.
Guilt comes next,
spurred from your intellectual drive
by deep thinking.
Veins of sublime contemplation pump
and when the blood pools,
it gives a bleak sense of hopelessness.
Every appendage of your body
becomes heavy and it's harder to move.

But the submissive seekers demur from this.
They believe in purity.
They inspire the minority to believe
that it must change.
A verve pulls them from the crazy machination of life.
Standing,
on a chessboard without pieces.
Where only the spaces move.
Every step is controlled by the board.
Not knowing
but believing
it possible
to overcome.

City Steps

The end of the week -
Glumly it grins without gumption.
City steps clap the pavement
creating a sordid melody of misery.

Intent on listening
I close my eyes,
I don't move.

What a city.
What a sad song.
What a strange way to soothe my soul.

Overthinking is a native casualty of living
in New York City.

Mistakes

There have been mistakes.
Unfortunately
There have been many.
I hope that you haven't collected as many.
I really don't hope that for you.

But,

if you have some, don't beat yourself up.
Don't pry into the past.
It's a delusional potion.

And,

if you let it,
it will linger within your veins.
It will enter into each organ,
and seep into your soul.

But,

stop it before it seeps into your heart.
Yes, mistakes can do that.

And,

I hope they are few and far between.
I hope you have the courage to forgive yourself.
I hope you can be brave,
because there will always be mistakes.

Pour it on me

The world isn't that hard.
It really isn't.
We make it more difficult.
This stems from
things we don't need,
places we'd rather be,
people we'll never be.

It's different for me.
It's different for us.
And the obstacles of our lives mean nothing.
They're a velveteen rabbit,
luring us away to a fanciful mirage of deceit.

It takes courage to be happy with your life.
It's okay to be happy.

Understand what you truly want
and never stop until you get there.
There are no rules to this game.
The points come before, during and after the match.
Sometimes points don't matter at all.

The world isn't too hard.
Envy and inferiority makes us the loser.
The winners never fight.
They know better.
If you still don't believe me, that's okay.
You just need to walk outside when it rains.
That's when things become clearer again.

The Loser

It had been 3 months since I last saw her.
I admit the collection of empty bottles and glasses
grew rapidly during that wrinkle in time.
I called and texted her in the late hours,
the context is never sincere,
the questions are always suggestive,
a, "Can I come over?"
or, "We should get together,"
her phone buzzing at the twilight hours of 12-3 a.m.

That must have infuriated her.
I'm repulsed by it.
But, even through my disgusting disregards,
she came one night.
She looked great,
just like she always did.

I wished we could have forgotten the bullshit,
a direct result of my past actions,
my selfishness
my burdens.
I wanted to forget everything and enjoy that night.

The bulbs along the bar's crossing beams hung low,
segmented sparkles blowing kisses
in the late summer's breathe.
She wasn't kissing me then.
She told me I was a loser,
a disappointment, and a complete waste of fucking time.
If she only knew how right she was.
I could have told her that the first time we met.

She was abrasive,
hoping to break me down.
It was a way for her to wiggle her way back in
and amend our discourse.
She held a hopeless belief that
we could see eye-to-eye.
Her approach disappointed me.
If only there had been more compassion,
maybe things could have worked.

People will say anything
to get back what was taken from them.
They do it to incite
a rise
a reaction
a test poised to oppress,
an evaluation of their rank.
It's hard to be defensive
when you're the weakest player on your own team.

I didn't say anything:
I was a loser.
I wondered if all this writing
I had collected was worth leaving,
or if she was right that I should continue.

I began to doubt myself.
She wouldn't understand.
She didn't know that she was only a fan.
She would never be happy dealing with me.
That's why I didn't let her.
Because I can't doubt myself,
and nobody really knows how to deal with anyone.
That, I'm sure of.

Maybe one day she'll read these damn words.
If I'm lucky they'll make sense of things.
Possibly she'll get the explanation she needs.
I hope she finds closure.
She'll know it is not worth dealing with a loser.

My life could be better, if I didn't have to live in it.

I Would Pay You My Soul, But We're Broke Baby

I'll admit it; I didn't make it easy for you.
No, I never knew myself well enough.
I could never decide who you were either.
I guess I relied on believing that
we were something to believe in.

Two years of this circus.
Two years of trying to fix something.
Two years of missing parts.
Two years of maintenance.
Two years...

I don't regret it.
I still remember the moment I fell for you.
That summer – I never felt more alive.

I looked into your face.
I wanted to look into it forever.

I'm not sure what would have changed
if I had stayed in Maine,
if I had stopped and returned back to the beach house.
The tears streaming down my face,
Atlas Hands buzzing in my ears.
The coolness of the window's glass was my only distraction.
I was scared shitless of what would happen
in New York, New York.
Everything changed.

You came for me – I knew you would.

But I didn't know you then.
We had to start over.
After learning about each other,
we found out that it wasn't right,
but we held on to that summer...

The on again, off again,
it left me blind.
I wondered each day whether I would be able to see.
I wanted us too – to see – to just see,
but I guess it's not that easy.

I worked, sacrificed and hoped for the best.
There were so many times that I wanted to quit.
But – I never felt so true with you.
I know you wanted to feel the same.
But – I never felt that you could.
You didn't seem ready.

You were a fragile fawn,
I wanted to make you stronger.
I needed you to feel stronger.

You can't be strong if the one you love is weak.

It takes strength to be alone.
I don't think either one of us had enough to be alone.
Well, until now.

My heart has a small tear in it.
It leaks from time to time.
It allows some of your love to leave.
That's something I'm still mending.

But –
I'm exasperated, tired and broke.

I have to move on

You have to move on.

I remember you in the light.
I selfishly want to forget the times I placed you in the dark.
I know you felt tormented.
I know you thought you were giving me everything.
I know you thought I wasn't.
And that's okay – because that is your right.

But please know I haven't forgotten your devotion.
How could I ever forget something as precious as that.

Fuck, this is shit!
There goes my temper again.
I would call you this moment.
I'd try again...
You would be here, I know it.
But I'm stopping now...
I need to stop...

I remember you two years ago.
I remember your dark hair.
I remember your perfect lips.
I remember your vulnerability.
I remember your face – forever.
I remember us falling for each other.
I remember your love
I remember our - no - I won't let myself go there.

For memory is nothing more than temporary bliss.

And I'm choosing to remember you tonight.

Look Right

It's been 5 years since I looked out
the left side of a car.
In cabs, I always sit so I can see Long Island City through
the cables holding up the Queensboro Bridge.
In the distance, almost touching the water,
the neon Coca-Cola sign bleeds
over Gantry State Park.

Roosevelt Island is hard to get to by subway.
So at lunch I take walks along 59th
and pass under large overhangs of bridges
built years before I was born.

I get to the water's edge,
and I reflect on it.
Boroughs divided by rivers and streams.
It is only here that I am able to look left.

Fickle Fools

We long to feel a sense of belonging.
So we trust each other easily.
It is in our nature.
An essential casualty of the human condition.

This leaves us susceptible to vulnerability,
bent and burned at times,
when gloomy skies are wished to bleed sunrays.

Everyone is too busy,
focused on distractions,
avoiding value and integrity,
and without theses we prance around the streets of Manhattan,
tricking ourselves.

If only we could realize how utterly restless we are.
It would help if we stopped for a moment
to think
to question
to admit something of substance.
But how can that happen?
We are nothing but fickle fools.

Hope and cynicism are like men and women,
compatible at wit's end.

A Shot To Forget The Loneliness

(New Year, Same Time)

The streets weren't for me last night,
but I walked them anyway.
The year passed
and I, well, I didn't know who I was becoming.
I had left my friends at the party
after we had taken one last shot.
One last sip, a celebration to forget.
Or at the very least
to mend the disappointments
that came from last year
that would come from this year.

And as I walked on the street,
I began to forget what to remember.
It didn't seem to matter then, or ever,
because remembering seemed to be
the worst part about it all.
I didn't feel bad about thinking about her,
but I did feel bad for thinking about her
while going to see someone else.
I kept walking hoping that the shot would take its toll.

14th and 3rd - I was halfway there.
I flagged the cab but it didn't stop,
its numbers dimmed.
I was too blind to know the difference.
Looking forward I saw a parade, a long line of loners,
a conglomerate of naysayers.
They were going to make the best of it tonight.
They were also trying to forget.
And I was forgetting.

Creeping slowly down the stairwell, all was clear.
I hid under the neon dry cleaning sign.
My shirt was dirty. I could've dropped it off.

The urine nearly hit my toes,
but I felt lighter then,
and it helped make my goal clearer.

I walked more quickly.
The arms of another naysayer were waiting!
I would be inside her soon.

The car swerved and nearly drenched me,
the puddles coming from a deep crevice in the pavement,
the taxpayer's dollars, well spent.

The confusion was tragic,
the numbers to the building were fuzzy to read.
Right side even - left side odd
Where the hell is 369 29th street?
I'm too tired for this.
I'm too drunk for this.
I'm too nostalgic... for her.

I stopped into a store and got provisions.
The condoms were required,
and I had to be sure to protect myself.
The party mix bag of chips - well that was for security.
Something to remind myself that I used to be young.
Things used to be less complicated.
One day, things will slow down.

To the 8th floor and I burst through.
The tree illuminated, the gifts gone from a week ago,
I peeked in the door.
The crunch of the pretzels woke her up.
I placed it down - the whole bag - and disrobed.
Slowly peeking underneath the covers,
just enough to startle the radiance of her nerve.
Neither of us knew what was happening,
but we were going to make it happen.

I slowly peeled her robe back
and I noticed she prepared for my arrival.

Naysayer within naysayer I thrust slowly,
holding to the bed's metal frame.
Patiently recounting the steps necessary for -
for the previous her.
It was working - but I was - I couldn't -
my mind was cluttered.
I didn't stop - I couldn't - It would be unfair.
But I didn't want it.

I slowly recoiled after her peak.
I refrained from self-indulgence.
I remained there.
With her - but wanting to be back on the street.
Walking - anywhere
Maybe back to the bar?
Back to the shots?
Back to where I didn't have to remember?

It was at that moment, with someone else,
that I couldn't,
I couldn't forget about her.

The Feather's Path

I think anyone anywhere can go where they want.
And, no, I don't mean within your mind.
No, that sways and flutters like a bird's loose feather.
It falls in areas dictated by the elements.
I'd rather grab the feather and
stick it where it needs to be.

It is peaceful,
like when you listen to a song
and start crying for no reason
other than finding it to be beautifully flawed,
just like you,
just like everyone.

It's better to just go with it.

Or like the sudden chill
experienced after listening to a voice's low tone
soothing you from everything that has stirred anxiety.
It doesn't matter and the goose bumps percolate,
and it's the only feeling that you want to have.
It's just perfect.
It's sad, but in the happiest way.

I wonder where the feather will fly next?
I'll follow the wind until I want to stop the feather's path.
Drifting - I am encumbered by
a course led by anything and anyone else.

Sex

Good sex is hard to come by.
It has nothing to do with the physical act of it.
Hell, it feels good no matter how bad or often it occurs,
and that's my problem.
It's only good if you feel comfortable.

I enjoy every aspect of two people coming together,
Vulnerable.
Desirous.
Where the good doesn't always fit.

The speed with which we have sex is too fast
too rapid
too short
too premature.
You laugh,
but it's for all the reasons that you shouldn't.

Have you ever had sex with someone
and immediately regretted it?
Have you ever had sex and wished you had waited?
Have you ever had sex and thought to yourself that you wished
you hadn't,
because you did it for the wrong reasons?
Maybe these questions come later
after the thrill of the act erodes away.

Lately, I feel like I've cheapened
myself and the women I've had sex with.
After it's over, no one says anything.
I do it because I don't want to get caught.
They don't because they know
that's exactly what I'm thinking.
I used to enjoy sex, even after it was over.
Now I enjoy it,
but afterwards, I can't wait for it to be over.

Sex, as a quick fix, is chronically blissless.
Lust is an obsession,
and it comes in the absence of validation.
So we go forth trying to find something that isn't there.
A self-serving reminder that we are desirable.

It's only when we wait,
when we take the time to overlook
the vanities associated with sex,
to trade one hundred nights of companionship
for one built-up night
when it's good,
when it's so good
that you'll never want to do it with anyone else.
It's hard to come by though.
Anything good is.

Magic
comes only after you've failed too many times
and your beauty
has no other option
but to set itself free.

Disguised By The Riot

There is always that small part.
It lingers unnoticed until the silky façade exposes itself.
It's the only thing that holds us back.

It causes fear.
It procures hesitation.
It could even be called a disease.

We can be completely lost by it.
If not for the fight,
we would be nothing.

We must fight it,
we must,
pushing aside the insecurities and the demons.

Take the chance.
Take the chance on yourself.
Take the chance on your friends.
Take the chance on your girlfriend or boyfriend.
Take it...

If you don't you'll have nothing.
It has nothing to do
with the admiration of the world.
It doesn't.
And if that is what you think it's all about then you're hiding.

Just let go.
Just let go.
Just let go.

Everything you could ever want will come.
You must allow it to come into your life.
And once you have, it doesn't waiver.

Don't abuse it: it's easy to push it away.
Cherish it.
It's the only responsibility worth having.
Only you can mess it up.

You may falter, but you can always reconcile.
Too many fallacies will rot the very being of its purity.
So be careful with what you have.
The worst place anyone can be
Is lost.

Little Nothings

There's a lot of loss,
Loss of friends
Loss of youth
Loss of opportunities
Loss of happy ones
Loss of sad ones
Loss

The streets carry that loss with us.
Faces looking for something,
a scrape
a scar
a stab
Anything to make us bleed with feeling again.
Perpetrated by the past's damnation,
a ticking time bomb collected from
the media
the government
the schools
the bosses
the girlfriends
the boyfriends

Everything takes us away
from where we're supposed to be.
It's no wonder we aren't given
a blank piece of paper and pen on the first day of school.

Why, how careless would it be to ask us to
write
draw
rip
demolish the paper?

To make choices,
that's all we're asking for.

The sky is full of stars in need of a friend.
They are waiting for someone to wish upon them.
Hopefully the one you choose doesn't fall,
mesmerizing the airways before it disintegrates,
an intergalactic firework,
a black nothing.

How beautiful it is to be so lonely.

Even explosions
at first
fill us up with hope.

Milk Run on 34th Ave.

(Astoria Calling)

The deli's sign is green with yellow letters.
I miss it,
the way it used to be,
when the background was yellow,
the words, red.
It used to be a shitty sign just a week ago.
I preferred it that way:
At least the deli looked aged,
Like it was some sort of landmark.
Now it looks new
and too polished.
The vegetables used to look suspect,
I would only buy the ones I needed.
They would last a day,
maybe a day and a half until they rotted.
Now, with the store's makeover,
those vegetables look fresher:
Yet another of life's optical illusions.

Alpha Laundromat is packed,
I don't have to walk in to know it.
The front windows are fogged.
I can't see inside,
but I know there are dirty quarters, fabric softener sheets and
heaps of cotton wear circulating within the sauna.
I wonder if any of the Hispanic kids
are running around inside.
Wait, there's one.
They tend to trickle away from their parents
and play on the sidewalk.
When a stranger approaches they run back inside.
They always stare at the stranger
right before going back in.
I've been stared at many times.

Grusko's is the saddest restaurant in the world.
It's not their fault though,
just a poor choice in location.
Isn't that something?

Astoria, basically New York City,
on 34th Avenue,
nearly a cross street to Steinway,
a bad location?
It is.
The huge dining room lies empty.
The waiter washes the same glass 10 times
throughout the night.
He's got nothing better to do.
Grusko smokes a fat cigar at the bar,
the giant Greek with caper-sized eyes.
Good for him, you couldn't see the sadness in them.
And even if you tried,
even if you got real close,
you still wouldn't be able to.
Your face would be blocked by a puff of smoke.

I pass by Willy.
He tries to snatch the air in front of him.
I wonder where he goes.
There's no way he sits outside the Rite Aid all day.
Not a bad place to be a bum, I guess.
At least you're near the essentials.
He's even got a magazine he uses for personal matters.
I glanced over at it just see that he's interested in
Black Booty.

I think of saying hi to Willy, but I don't.
Who knows what he'll do or say?
I'd feel obligated to give him money, food, or a moment of time
to listen.
So I don't start.
If I do it once, I'll have to do it every time.
Even if I don't want too,
I'll have too.
I don't blame Willy.
No, I don't
He's human.
He's fragile.
He's just trying to make a connection.
He's just like everyone else.

You know how it goes.
Once anyone gives someone a chance they hold on to it.
I guess I'm not giving Willy a chance.
The effort comes with a personal consequence,
but I don't have time right now,
I need to get milk.

When all hope is gone,
a small amount remains in a crevice
you forget to look in.

Three's a Crowd

On top of the heap.
I'm no longer a climber.
I'm standing at the peak.
Another girl,
another night,

Then it changes.
The glamour dissipates
like the puddles into drains,
sluggishly roaming the streets,
trying to find its escape.

It's sad sometimes to think about it that way,
but even water, pure water, becomes polluted.

I've tried to dilute myself.
I'm not sure if I've tried hard enough.
Those girls are going to get hurt,
they are.
The worst thing about it:
It'll be because of me.

I'm feeling high right now,
but soon
it'll come.
I'll return to the base.
I'll be happy again.

The purity in anything
comes from those who are climbing.
Once you've reached the top
you can't see things the same.
You can't see others,
you just see yourself.

Iceman

When my confidence suffers
I'm melting ice.
Down
Down
Down
I go.

The puddle.
Two eyes float,
wishful.
I hope I can pull it together.
I'd do anything to be whole again.

The beat of my soles slows.
I need something,
anything
to get me up.
Slippery and sunken.

Heat?
No, I can't face it.
I'd evaporate

unless the clouds cool
and I come back.
Drops drizzle.
They break like disorder upon the glass windows,
cleaving
a slow, silky ride down to the base.

Bear upon the world again.
All I need is a cool night.
It will build me up.
And it always comes,
I just don't know when.

I cross the street
the next morning.
A puddle.
I jump over it.
Looks like that guy didn't make it past lunch.

An Apology Note That Wasn't Worth Sending

I'm having a real hard time with this one. I mean, I know that I just met you and like we hardly know one another. But I always have a hard time finding people that not only get me, but also embrace me with open arms. I tend to be alone a lot - I've always been that way. I guess it's a defense mechanism: when you're alone – well, you don't have to worry about being hurt. But after meeting you, I feel different. In a strange way I feel like you know me better than most of my friends - I guess that's making a connection; I haven't experienced that for some time.

The emotional rollercoaster started when I first left you: "Finally, I found someone that I can be around and feel like myself."

And now the last time I left you, "Why did this have to happen, why, just why."

It's usual to be guarded, to question who the hell someone really is. It's made worse when they act crazy or make mistakes, because we're all vulnerable - and we all want to avoid feeling hurt. I know you're hurt from the other night. I can't stress how bad I've felt. And I feel ill at times because of how it must have affected you.

For me, mistakes happen: we mess up, but what really gets to me is that if we just drop this thing we might both miss an opportunity to be with someone who could put us at ease. And that's where the wonder sets in - and I know that, for you, the desire to wonder has been subdued, it has been squashed into a little crevice of your mind.

But me, my heart still pounds with wonder.

We're all searching for some peace of mind - and I'll admit, after meeting you I hadn't found that yet: it was too early. I was caught up in the excitement and anxiety of everything, of you, your grace, things we could do together.

The anxiety is, as you could probably tell, one of my shortcomings. It's difficult because I was so eager to be around you - but then I worried that I would find something about you that would turn me away, or that I would be exposed as someone you wouldn't want in your life, or that I would do something to mess the whole thing up.

I've dated other girls in the city, and to be completely honest, if something like this happened with them, I would feel bad - I truly would. I mean I grew up with all women, so I know that every one of them should be treated with the respect and care they desire.

Just like you.

But like I was saying - if this happened with someone else, I would apologize, but probably I would leave it. I wouldn't press to speak to her again. It's different with you: I know I just met you, but I'm sure you've dated enough people to know, when you find a good connection with someone, someone who matters, you try, if you're like me, you try to salvage those relationships because they're rare, amazing, and completely scary, all at the same time.

I wasn't expecting this at all last week. I almost didn't go over to Jerry and Matt's place - but I did - and I met you. For me, sitting on the couch and being at the bar Friday were the best parts: we talked - we just talked. I have a hard time speaking with girls at times; I tend to shy away from the real me and play the humorist in the room. That night, I did less acting and instead opened up to you very quickly - and it seemed you did the same with me.

That's something - and it is/was/will be very special to me.

Aside from that, I of course think you are extremely attractive and sensual - I hope you know that as well. That is an important aspect to all of this. And I think that my oversight here may have been misleading. I did not intend for it to be: it was purely out of genuine respect for you – I would never want you to feel as though I presumed to have the privilege of touching your body.

I'm sorry for the length of this note, but this is how I tend to flush out my emotions: at night, alone, when my daily distractions fade away, and I'm finally able to reflect on my feelings.

I don't know where we stand. I mean we've barely started walking - but if you'll have me, I would like to get back up and slowly get back on track until we're running together.

With sincere regret and an optimistic outlook,

Joe

A leather-bound notebook
isn't required to be creative;
a pen and loose sheets of paper
work just as well.

The Man I Used To Be

To be true to himself,
that's all a man can do
or ask of himself.

Without that,
well, you are only playing a role.
Someone else's part supersedes your desire.

When you look into your own eyes
make sure you see the man you're supposed to be.
That's the only thing in the world
that you have control over

It really is

It's the only thing that you can hold sacred

I hope I can be true again – yes – I have faith that *I* will.

Netflixinitis

Never has society been more of a watcher.
Staring needlessly at devices.
A hobby based on a distraction.
A filler for thought.
"I've got to watch my show."

Entertainment has nothing to do
with your viewing allegiance.
It comes from those who become inspired
to be greater than themselves
through the mediums that call to them,
not the animosity of those that have
dared to try
dared to fail
dared to succeed

Yes, people,
it's
hard
scary
and the wolves will eat you

Don't watch that next episode,
create one.

Dancing With Words

Sometimes I lead.
Sometimes they lead me.
The sentence structure is the least of my worries.
Though I could study form forever,
I'd get caught up in the steps if I did.
Toes and tabs would pinch.
So I work with the words,
I get to know them.

I subdue my excitement about
where the dance may take us.
I would lose out if only I led.
The words are just as important as my intention.
They were created to help me speak.

So I follow the cursor.
The white page fills.
Every step forward feels
as right as a surprise twist.
A sequence turns and builds up.
Our recital helps to create a marvelous...
Story

And once it's over,
when the words and I depart.
The dance is left on the page.
It lasts for a lifetime.

Let's drink the drink, and shoot the shit.

Finders Keepers

Sometimes I wish I never had anything at all.
It would be easier that way.
No bills
No apartment
No job
No friends
No girl
No ambition
No drive

If you have nothing, then you can be free.
Maybe it's not all as good as it appears.
That's the trouble I guess.
It's all about the urgency in knowing.
That part gets us all.
Once you lose anything
You'll want it back.

That's why we must believe in what we have.
But is it enough?
It seems that it's an unwinnable battle.
But like everyone else,
I don't know how to do anything,
but I expect to have it all.

Promotion

The review went flawlessly.
We acted exactly as we were supposed to.
No one flinched while the trivial banter
overrode my mediocre accolades.
The integrity of the center
echoed like hyenas laughing.
An inebriating cadence of bullshit.
Bullshit, yeah, sheer bullshit.

Promotion

And I sat – again – taking in the false security
of working for someone who doesn't give
a shit about me.
But I work.
I need the money.
I need to do something.
I'm nearing complacency and falling for its trick.
But doesn't this job mean something?
I need that security,
a job,
something that defines my existence.
The goal of another calendar year:
perfect attendance.

Promotion

Calculated by the mastermind of arrogant farts,
the CEO and his henchmen – the algorithm of worth:
the value of a man broken down to statistics,
the value of a man brought down to money,
the value of a man – despite his strife – despite his integrity,
the value of a man belittled by those
who are smaller than he.

Promotion

Falsely blissed by my own insecurities,
falling for the mirage,
misguided by untrue acceptance.
Does it really matter if I feel belonged?
Doesn't being alone justify its meaning?
Doesn't the value of a man alone
to himself
mean something?
The pixels filter on the screen
a spectacle of colors creates the images.
I stare at the images.
I look at the clock:
364 days left,
unless this is the last time,
unless I make this the last time.
But I don't know how to make it the last time.
So, until next year.

Promotion

Transient Companionship

Some will leave.
Actually, most will leave.
I know it's discouraging.
The mundane movement of life
is better with the company of friends.
The grandest of events that you dream for yourself
will never compare to the sincerity of joint experience
with others.
It will end
and you'll be mad.
You'll wish you never had such great times together.
It'll hurt like the worst stomachache you've ever had.
I can tell you to not be sour,
but I've known that pain.
Alone for a long while.
Wondering
why did everything change?
Why have you changed?

We're leading a life based on a distant memory.

Casting a line to catch something that seemed perfect.
But nothing is perfect.

Companionship comes back to those willing to let it in.
It's only a matter of time before you're back among them.
You feel whole again.
It's enough to keep you going.
It's enough to keep your friends going.
It's just enough.
And you're lucky to get any at all.

Mad moments
remind us
that no matter how bad it gets,
magic is waiting.

Dreaming While Awake

We were all laughing.
The hours were passing by as smoothly as the Cabernet.
I kept swirling,
transfixed as it laced around the walls of my glass,
the legs of the liquid streaking down
to the red sea of nevermore.

Here come the European girls.
Last time they were Spanish,
and the time before that they were Russian.

I can't remember anything they said.
The cigarette smoke prohibits one
from reading lips.
The local dialect muddles.
Soon, they sound all the same.

It's like this every night.
It's been like this for the past three years.

"The next round is on me!"
The next, next round – when it comes – it'll be on me.
It doesn't matter if anyone asks permission to use my tab.
I don't know the last time
I said, 'No.'

So the goes night.
We sleep while awake,
living in darkness,
a searing reality based a on vibe.

In the morning,
we try to recall anything.
Anything that we lived through.
Anything that we forgot.
Anything we dreamed.

But it is becoming harder and harder
to tell the difference.

Go to Music

There are some songs that let you cry.
There are some songs that let you laugh.
There are some songs that let you relax.

But,
when a songs hits you,
when it creates a sense of relief,
like the weights of life have been lifted,
a tempest cools within,
a rain shower falls,
a rainbow appears,
crystal clear,
a foreign vision of beauty.

There's a song out there.
Listen.
Play it on repeat.
Close your eyes.
Allow the dreams of yesterday
or the ones from 5, 10, 20 years ago pass through.
Serene solitarily.
Followers of crowds will only attempt
to grasp something like this.

Be alone with your song.
Allow the melody to infiltrate the veins of your body.
The blood surging to every part
of your body's capacity.
The oxygen will bring in new life.
The chill of liberty destroys conformity.
It's the only thing that'll keep you alive at times.
There's nothing better than letting go.

Don't Gloat About The Goat

You won't want to hear it.
You really don't.
Yes, you think you'll want to hear it.
You've worked so hard.
You've tried to impress everyone.
But you won't want to hear it.

I've heard it many times.
I've felt the elation,
The acceptance,
The sweet serenity of it all.
I've felt the sky.
I've shaken hands with the clouds.

But you won't want to hear it.
It's fluff, you know,
a compliment.
It's corn feed.
It's their way of telling you that you're below them.
But I don't eat corn anymore.

I don't need it.
I don't want it.
I know what I've got.
I know it's beyond their capacity.
I know
I know

You'll know.
Don't listen to them.
Don't rely on them.
Don't change for them.
Listen,
but only to yourself!

You've got
the goods
the passion.
It's all in you.
It has always been in you.
Start now.
Start again.
Just start.
Just do it all ready!

Waiting will only make it leave.
And if you wait,
don't talk to me anymore.
I don't need you to become like the rest.
I don't.
You don't.
Just do it.
Don't stop until it's done.
Don't gloat that it's almost done.
Don't praise yourself until you know it's finished.
Finish already!
Finish.
God damn it!
Finish.

When you do – you'll be sad.
You won't want to be done.
You don't want it to be over.
It was everything to you.
It was a part of you.
That's when you know it is right.
That's when you'll see all the dicks and assholes
were just idiots all along.
They could never make
what you have created.

Fuck them.
Fuck them all.
Just fucking believe that you and only you can do it.
Because you were born to do it.
You were made to do it.
Afterwards,
don't say a word.
Be silent.
Know that it's done.
It doesn't matter if anyone else knows.
It doesn't.
It really doesn't.
It only matters to you.

I can't speak without a voice.
I can't listen without hearing.
I can't feel without writing.

Nervous

It rises again.
My heart is pumping.
Smoke is coming out of my ears.
My breath is forced.
Sometimes I wish the fire could be calmed.

But it will always be there:
the job
the women
the shitty writer's block
even the fucking subway

There's always something there.
I could leave it all I guess.
Then,
the anxiety,
the disappointment,
and the self-doubt would leave.
I suppose that would be the easy way out,
the easiest way to run from frustration.

My stomach could calm like a lake,
and no longer crash with raucous waves.
I'd find peace of mind.
I could finally sleep
and sleep.
Only sleep.

It would be colder then.
I wouldn't have the job.
I wouldn't have the women.
I wouldn't need to write.
I would be cold.

I don't want to freeze,
even if being warm makes me lose it all.
And so,
it rises,
like it always does.
There is nothing I can do about it.
And so,
I keep writing.

The Trouble In NYC

New York City can be a real shit hole.
I mean what's a guy to do?
If he's looking for trouble he doesn't have to look far.

Most of the time it'll find him.
The city feeds on that,
in some ways it profits from it.

The trouble,
I think that's what it's all about.

I'm writing this at 6am.
I can't even look outside the window yet.
Seriously, an ambulance has just stopped
in front of my apartment.
Blue and red lights dance over my face.
Talk about a distraction.

The trouble
and more will be waiting for me.
Might as well take a shower first.
No,
fuck it.
I don't feel like it today.
And besides,
who's going to know the difference?

Eyes

She sat across from me.
Her eyes were shadowy beads
that gleamed blue against the light.
There was a lot in those eyes.
I saw a lot of hope from the start.

There were other things.
I could see times of sorrow.
I could see times of pain.
I could see hurt in those eyes.
What I saw most was a sense of protection.

I knew she was considering letting me in,
but it would take time,
a small opening.
It came every so often.
And as my eyes widened
I could see her eyes become less welcoming,
like gates to a castle.

She wasn't sure if she wanted me to come in.
Guards were ready.
I knew I wouldn't make it tonight.
That was okay,
I wasn't ready to ambush.

Maybe I could try the next time,
or maybe this was the only chance I would get.
I wanted to reach her.
But it wasn't up to me anymore.

As she left,
there was one last memory.
Her storming black hair whipped
and she looked back.
I saw the blueness in her eyes grow.
I wasn't there yet.
I wasn't.

If I waited,
I would be,
I will be soon.

Drips instigate madness,
it just takes a big one
to drive me insane!

Put It On The Line

(Newfound Success, Excusable Bad Habits)

"There is something about that guy"
"He really has it all together"
"When he enters the room, the entire mood changes"

I've heard these things said about me.
I guess it's what they think of me.
There may even be some envy.
But for me,
the guy they think has it all together.
Well,
I envy them.

They don't have to worry
or walk into a room feeling ill,
scared to mess up.
Every sip I take is followed
quickly by another.

I can't help but feel out of place.

And as I force a smile and continue the banter
throughout the room,

I don't want to mess up

I desperately hope I don't.
Sip
Sip, sip
Sip. sip , sip.
Okay boy you're doing well.
It's getting foggy
and I should be on my guard
But I'm not.

This is where heroes turn into villains.

Hugs and cheek kisses are exchanged.
I'm holding on to the last glass.
The bartenders know my name by now.
They bend the rules and pour one last hurrah.
I wish they wouldn't,
but it's not their fault.

I've tricked them,
or maybe I'm trying to trick myself.

I walk into the cool night.
The bustling streets filled.
The city looks like it always does:
a cocktail of two mixed poisons,
Hope and despair.

The yellow cab comes and picks me up.
I could go to Tuttles.
Shane would have the Malbec ready for me.
I consider,
but I'm good tonight.

I'm lucky tonight.

Back to Astoria.
Back to myself.
The show is over.
The curtains have closed.
I sit in my apartment.
I'm content.
I'm at ease.

The next show is tomorrow.
I have to be ready for it.
I hope I hit my cues.
I hope I can adapt.
I hope I don't let them down.

I hope I can remain the hero.

Pond

(Alcohol Paradise)

There's an allure,
a temptation.

A pond.

We think it's easy to step in.
So we touch the water.
We like the feel.
It's unusual.
We feel as if we're part of something great.

The greatest grandeur.

Leg deep.
Waist deep.
Deeper and deeper.

So deep that we are consumed.

If we're lucky, we remember.
We jump up.
It's only then we can breathe again.

So we rush out.
Dry, we are comfortable.
Shivering, we watch.

The smooth glaze of the water ripples like silk.

It's a song to some.
They lean in to hear better.
It sounds so lovely.

Impervious, we forget our inhibitions.

We pretend to think the pond gives us what we need,
everything we've ever wanted.

So we take that first step.
And then, the next.
And the next.
We feel the pond's gravity more and more with each.

Just like last time.

One day we stop moving.
Our last breath leaves.
Overpowered by circumstance.
It's then that the shore doesn't seem so plain.

If only we didn't allow ourselves to drown.

If we'd known to admire the pond from afar.
We could have remained safely on shore.

Coffee Spill

A girl on the train spills her coffee,
a full one.
A puddle of brewed, brown bean
mixes with the cream.
It lies between her feet.
She looks on with the other passengers
as a massive stream outstretches
like roots under a tree.
Toes tip near the edge of caffeine.
The girl sits with a bitchy face.
She looks sideways,
positions her glasses more appropriately on her nose.
Others offer scowls.
She acts as if she does not notice,
chooses instead to take no sugar
as she deals with today's misery.

Be you, be better and be beautiful.

If You Must

If you must tell her - really tell her.
If your heart is pounding
because your veins are surging with it,
then tell her.
If swallowing food would be difficult,
tell her.

If you're not sure,
don't tell her.
If you plan to tell her
because that'll get you a good lay,
don't tell her.
Lying clips wings.
Too many men, ready to fly, remain grounded.

She doesn't want now, she believes in forever.

But if you tell her, be prepared.
She may not tell you back.
She may not be ready.
But if you have to tell her - say it.
Say it.
Say it before someone else does.
And there will be someone else.
They're lurking alone right now,
envisioning your girl.
Say it,
if you really mean it.

If she decides to leave after you say it,
let her.
Don't fight to tell her again.
Don't be persuasive.
She knows what you said.
She knows what you meant.
She's been waiting to hear it her whole life.
Take a chance though.
It's the only good one you'll have.

But why take the chance?
What if she doesn't say it back?
What if she does say it back?
What if she does?

Allow your wings the ability to flap.
Your heart will surge.
Your vision will be clear.
Everything will become euphoric.
It's better than
money
fame
or having a beautiful woman...
that is never ready to soar.

If she says it,
you must protect it,
you must cherish it.
Because after you tell her,
you have to show it.
And show it!
If you don't,
It will all seem to be a lie.

And if you lie,
you'll make it harder for guys like us.
You'll make it hard for us to tell her.
So if you must tell her – be ready to show her.

Holy Shit

We try to fix mistakes,
the mistakes we've made today,
the ones made yesterday,
and the worst ones,
the deep-seated mistakes,
rooted down beneath our bellies,
come back to us
in moments when we thought we had forgotten.

It makes sense that we'd want to get rid of them.
Cleansed
Saved
Like religion, I guess.
A source of belief.

But I don't believe in higher powers.
No, I think it is a scam.
A way to capitalize on the raw emotions of humanity.
A ploy to market salvation.

There's only one person who can save you,
and,
reciting scriptures or holding your hands together won't connect
him - her - it - to you.
It's a mental choice.
One that comes from self-forgiveness.
One that doesn't require some display of devotion.
It could occur when you're
brushing your teeth
or eating a hotdog,
or, Hell, while watching a dog shit.

Yes, you were created by some miracle,
but those people or holy enigmas don't make you.
Nor do they affect
your decisions,
your beliefs.

The mistakes will come.
They'll pile up just as life intends them too.
It's your choice to move on.
Only you can pick up the broom
and sweep them away.

Pretty Flawed

Some people can be so gorgeously flawed.
It can be hard to tell at first.
It must be hard for them.
I bet they wish someone could fix them.
Who do you know
who would ever admit to that?
No one, I guess.
They move on looking as elegant as ever,
wondering how they ever got there.
How does someone get there in the first place?
It's sad, really.
But they wake up to a new day,
incongruously living within society's accolades,
helpless by their impression,
and yet, pretty as hell.

*I don't want to
hear stories,
I want to
tell them.*

Leaves

I like being sad... sometimes.
It's the only time I know I still have a pulse.

Raw emotion can be just as reclusive as humility.
Buried under the mountains of fall leaves,

waiting for winter's kiss,
leaves iced under flakes,

hidden from all subjectivity,
I appear like everyone else.

I wait for the spring,
the sadness.

It's allowed to melt,
the leaves soiled.

It's time to rake.
I can see clearly

until next fall,
and fall is always approaching.

Broken Glass

I forgot to put the dirty glass in the sink.
Friggin' ey! - I'm sitting in my chair,
ready to watch a movie.
I should get the glass.
I really don't want to.
My mind flutters to tomorrow's tasks,
the menial duties that daunt us,
piled up, waiting for the shovel.

The damn glass stares at me.
It sits on the bar cart's right-upper ledge.
It's not a big deal
but I'm using it
as an excuse for everything else.

Sometimes I wish I had the guts
to pick the glass up and throw it against the wall.

You know, a way to let a little steam out.
I'd watch the cylinder effervescently glide thru the air towards the
wall and shatter with the sweet sound that breaking glass makes.
A splat, crack and chime.
Glass beads would cascade to the floor - each one creating a
symphony of tones,
a melody unique to the forces
of heaving crystallized shards.

I wish I had the guts to do a lot of things.

But I already have enough to worry about.
I'll get the glass tomorrow before I leave for work.
If I forget, I'll deal with it later on.

Young Company

I surround myself with young company
to forget about my fragility.
Aging isn't something I fear.
It's the effects of age that worry me.
I'm scared I'll forget what it's like to be fresh.
So I surround myself with young company.

They aren't transfixed by unrest.
There's ambition inside their souls.
They haven't been let down enough to feel guilt.
There's an inert community
and they float as seamlessly as clouds in the sky,
adjacent to the vibrant blue background
as white wisps of pure innocence.

I'm pushing thirty.
My hair has thinned.
Hell, I know I'll lose it all soon.
My gut widens more quickly than it used too,
the hangovers last much longer than a day,
yet this doesn't cross the minds of young company.

Although they may joke about my age,
and even if I look like the creepy guy
that needs to grow up,
they know it's different.
They see it in my eyes.
The fearless delusion of a man pressing on,
refusing to let the world get to him.

When I see a change in their eyes,
typically when least expected,
when the quit overtakes the fight,
when the howlers quit howling,
that's when I have to find new company.
I can't be around anything else.
I can't.
I just can't.

I'll always be around young friends.
I live off their fervor for chaos.
I struggle to be more calculated,
because even with my wisdom,
I can't help getting caught up in their unruliness,
for which their naivety excuses them.
Sometimes, even when I know
I should abide by society's rules,
I trick myself, wanting to feel
a sense of invincibility again.

I let myself believe.
Otherwise, there'd be very little left.
I'd become just like those people that look back.
I'd decide that those times have passed by.
Reminiscent...
You wouldn't want to be around if that happened.
You could never bear the sight of my saddest eyes.

So I hold on.
The thrill of discovery outweighs
reaching the final destination.
And that's why I find myself around young company.

The story never ends.

Everyone is slightly phony,
remember that,
and you'll go far.

The Sun Will Come Out Tomorrow

Like the gloomy overcast,
a blanket of gray easily hides my fortitude.
Today I woke up to a clear sky.
The sun shone on my face.
I didn't want to hide anymore.

Running From The Madness In Me

(Radical Moment Of Melancholy)

I guess we all can be selfish,
but for fuck's sake,
doesn't that make sense?
The world, our lives,
It can all be real shit.

I wake up sometimes hoping that I can't smell or taste.
It'd be better that way:
I wouldn't have to gag
on the malodorous pheromones of despair, deceit and unfulfilled
expectations.

I hope there'll be sunnier days.
Yes, I'm aware how dramatic this passage is.
I hate writing it,
but I'm having a moment here.
A Shit!
Fuck!
Moment

Charging towards the Queensboro Bridge,
Crescent Avenue is always on my route.
I keep it consistent.
I walk alone.
I'm happy about that.

I don't want anyone to see me this way.
I could cry right now; legit tears are forming.
I shouldn't – I won't – but for some reason I want too.
If anyone saw me like this,
they'd never want to be around me.

But why?

Don't we all feel low sometimes?
We do - but like hell do we say anything about it.
I'm taking a deep breath.

I'm running and my mind is following my pace.
I'm okay, I'm okay.
For now.

That's the best I can do.
That's the best anyone can do.
My feet are barely touching the pavement,
but they feel like they're still going.
And I'm not sure
that I care
for how long.

The Greek Food Near Astoria-Ditmars Stop

The food looks the same.
I've been here over two hundred times.
I don't know what it is, but today, it's different.

I'd give anything to walk under the sky of lights,
holding her hand,
even though I'm sure...
- But maybe I was wrong.
I don't care who's right anymore.

I see things differently.
I'm a cyclical renegade waiting for the next thrill.
Now, I'm more assured –
or at least trying
to convince myself that I am.
It's easy to fall for a fantasy.

I can only move so fast.
My hands can grab only so many pieces,
and I want to hold her.
Maybe she's the only one I really need in the end.
At least when she's around, the food tastes better.

Poems
valiantly express
the ambiguity
in life.

Exhaustion Dabbed In Pretension
(Glazed by Incongruity)

The greatest thing to know is that you're safe.
But it sure as hell is difficult to feel that way.
A predicate formed by an illusion.
You fall victim to it.
Slowly, you'll creep back,
no longer fooled by illusions.
It all too soon becomes the same for everyone:
a desperate dissonance
entering into the fragility of your insecurity.
The victim of inhibition,
you can challenge it.
You should, but it's exasperating,
your confidence crippled by residual fear.
The nascent fright bears its teeth.
It will be the only thing that smiles,
chagrinned by the defeatist's in your mind.

Between The Lines

Everything has its framing,
structured to fit exactly as it should.
I never seem to be the one that stays within the lines.
But I guess – at times – you need to.
There's a grimace that comes with this conformity.
The black lines don't appear to guide.
No, instead they restrict,
an obstruction pushing you towards insanity.
To heavy drinking.
To loneliness.
To writing.

Moving you to a place far away
from those living with limits.
If only they ventured to the surrounding white spaces.
Dare to go there.
Don't let fear put you in a cage,
like the tiger at the zoo,
a beast that has the ability to roar.
A beast, when chained, only watches.
Dream for a better day.
Dream to wake up.
Dream to be different.
Cast away everything that binds you.

It takes a wild beast to be free,
and most of us have the ability to scream.

Stuck

You are not stuck.

I know during the day-to-day you see yourself
in places,
in jobs,
or with someone you don't feel is right.
You may think you can't get out.

You are not stuck.

You can get out.
You can move.
You can quit.
You can break things off.
You are the only one who can make this decision.
The woes of change are the only thing
holding you back.
Take the ride of chance.
Find the open lane.
Throw out the map .
Life is a chaotic highway.

It's never too late to start again.

Religion is a scam.
they should give the money to a worthy cause.
But, then again,
that probably would be another scam.

The Rattle Inside

My full head
is buried by too many thoughts
for any man to comprehend.

How can I pick
or focus on one.

Just an abundance of potentials,
with more clouding my vision.
Today's stimulus creates a new rattle for the storm.

Led Back To The Start

The A train rumbled on the tracks.
Rockaway wasn't in sight,
but we were nearing Utica Ave.
I was anxious.
I wasn't sure I even wanted to be there.
I sipped the Beck's out of the
large Dunkin Doughnuts Coffee mug.
It relaxed me.
I didn't even care that we had been traveling
for over two and a half hours.

I sat reeling from the night before -
the Fourth of July.
The beast in the sky was laughing last night.
It was all so blurry to me.
It seemed like the sky was on fire.
I watched from a stranger's stoop.
I was miserably warm the entire time.
The texts and the phone calls.
The desire to be with someone... anyone
But I didn't join anyone last night.
I thought about the girl I wanted,
how she didn't want me back.
And the ones who did
I couldn't want them either.
I didn't know myself.
I'm scared of change.
Being on the verge of becoming a man
has been weighing on me.
The decade of relinquished chaos
has come to a close this summer:
the parties, the drinking, the brattiness,
unabashed disregard for the establishment,
the fight that never gains victory.

Cynthia didn't know it,
but she reminded me of all of this
while we were on the train,
and she didn't know that I was taking her back to a place that
epitomized my twenties.

Youth holds a certain vision that loses itself
in those who resist it.
I was learning how much I resisted many things.
My opportunities
My friends
Myself
I got it back from time to time
but it seemed easier to just throw it all away.

Broadway Channel and we needed to transfer.
Cynthia was complaining about her boyfriend.
I listened,
but realized she was talking about someone like me.

"Man" is a scary thought for boys.

It isn't cute to be a boy forever,
no matter how hard you try.
Maybe I was being too hard on myself.
Or maybe I was going through the motions again.
Self-depreciation can be easily assuaged
if you're convincing.
The sting only lasts until you rub it away.
It stays though.
I, especially, seemed to be prone to more attacks.
And I didn't want it to stop.
I was used to it.
I, well, I guess I needed it.
At least then it would remind me
that I wasn't getting old and boring.
I need a stimulus, person, or situation
to deal with at every waking moment.
Then, when I awoke with the gut-wrenching feeling of apathy, I'd
completely abate my involvement.
Until I felt up for it all again.

That's why we went to Rockaway.
I'd always felt something there.

Looking Like Hell

I walked into work tired –
and what's worse
was how tired I looked.
I couldn't conceal the four hours of sleep.
The late alarm.
The lack of shaven skin.
"You'll kill yourself if you don't get healthy."
Thanks, co-worker with 3 kids.
"Death, you say?"
Seemed like a blessing.
At least I could rest.
Staying up until 2, 3 a.m. wasn't conducive to a 9-5
That's the problem with ambition:
the stubborn soul can't be appeased by failure.

Success won't kill ya –
the ambition to get there will.

So on with the job.
On with the long nights typing.
On with the mistakes that I haven't realized yet.
'Cause the shine gleams on those who are ready for it.
The rest remain in the shadows,
and I refuse to be cast into Hell's darkness.

I can't help but be enamored of every disgusting aspect of New York City.

The Rage Will Rise

I know it's there.
I like to think it leaves.
I like it when the boil simmers
and settles to calm water.

But the tide is elegantly waiting.
Chaos is near.

Smooth now, I am in complete control,
but I can't control the tide.
It ticks like a beast awaiting its prey.
Waiting to explode.

It comes at my most vulnerable moment.
I'm weak and I know it.

The wave rises.
I crash into myself.
Everyone else around me watches in disappointment.
It doesn't stop.

It can't be stopped.
Everything about me is wrong.
But my strength has never been more alive,

like the boxer. He waits for the right moment.
His excuse is to pulverize
the opponent...
his rage...
his fear...
his impossibilities...

The powerful prevail over what they can control.
I'm out of control again.

I hate it, but it must come out.
Yes, yes – it must.
If not, the storm will be larger next time.

If You're Distracted, Then You're Like Everyone Else

Maybe we seek distraction.
It gives us an agent to derail our real intentions.
It allows us to escape
from finding out who we really are.
In these moments,
It's effortless.
You don't have to face anything.
It keeps you from facing your fears.
And you'll never feel more lost unless you stop it.
But even when you act like there's time left,
and like you will "get there when you're ready,"
You'll miss out.
You'll never truly know your capabilities
because you're too distracted to find out otherwise.

Her, Recurring

It's sort of disgusting.
It's sort of beautiful.
It's sort of horrid.

In every way,
it's sort of perfect.

But the Hell with it.
The Hell with it all.
I don't give a damn any more.
Unless I have some inexplicable reason not to feel.

And fuck it.
When she is around,
when she isn't around,
I do feel.

I remember her.
I miss everything.
Even the bad parts.
And so,
I write to remember her.

*Restless tendencies turn into
reckless melodies.*

Acting In Reality

It's happening again
and I can't believe I'm allowing it.
Every creation
Every part of me
Everything is being taken away
And I let it be.
The damn boss steals it with a smile.
The paycheck is steady though.
Doesn't it always come down to money?
I feel like I've been bought.
I'm sure you feel the same.
It's sick – yes, almost ill fated,
a proverbial demise.
Our souls are diluted, ridiculed and left questioning.
Work is a personal purgatory
that cages our mounting disappointment.
It's hard to loosen control, but we allow for it.
Crumpled by the realization of doing something
below our potential.
But we clock in.
The bills are paid,
and after we clock out,
while we are on the commute home,
we wonder,
"How can we become whole again?"
"How can we be part of something
we no longer believe in it?"
But we act, our cubicle the main stage,
a small area designated
to meager our thoughts.
We work for individuals that could never
comprehend the beauty
that is really inside you, me and everyone else.
Slowly, like pebbles on a beach there's decay.
The salt and tide effacing
our ever-thinning integrity
until we become too fragile,
and turn into sand
lying on the beach's endless coastline.

Grin

Traveling home from work,
I gripped the rail of the N-train and watched her.
She stood nibbling her lower lip.
A disconcerting face,
every crevice is like a network of roots.
Her wrinkles dug deeper and deeper into the soil.

She probably was thinking the same thing I was:
another day dedicated to dumbasses.
I wasn't happy at all,
my talents wasted,
punching the keys of the keyboard
at my desk next to the repairman,
the radiator rings like Sunday church chimes,
my temporal lobes rattle,
thinning my resistance.
I should be so frenzied.

Another day,
and I'm packed into the train,
a slew of blank faces
all dealing with the same damn complex.

The woman looked at me briefly.
She released her lips.
Maybe it was a mutual understanding.
Or maybe she could tell by my face
that I needed it.
She smiled:
a curt grin, but nonetheless soothing.

It reminded me that we are all in it,
this shit life of labor:

together,
even if we are miserable as hell.
So I smiled back.
It felt good to do that.
I should smile more often.
We all should.

Rejection feeds the strength to prove the world wrong.

Drinking Fate

Fate

      is

           a

               drink

                    that

                        doesn't

                   end

               until

          the

      next

morning.

It'll take time,
it'll take longer than you think,
it'll take longer than you thought,
it'll take you to points where you're ready to quit,
but if your stamina can master the set-backs
you'll know exactly how long it took to get there.

City Noise

There is noise.
Always.
Even in the quiet moments of solitude.

The humming radiator.
The drops of water from a faucet.
The trash can top rattles.

The mind.
Thoughts of tomorrow.
Thoughts of yesterday.
Thoughts of days to come.
And what's worse... unexpected noises.

Caught by surprise.
Gasping for the chance to quiet it all.
Seeking a sense of control.
Unable to.

You'll have to get used to it.
I'd advise you to do so.
Because it's always going to be loud.
Louder... LOUDER.

Noise persists like the air you breathe.
It's at the times when you hold your breath,
that you can hear the silence.

The Keys Move

My writing process?
I tend to wait.
I start by writing words down.
Words I hope will take off.
Powerful - sad - loving - longing - wanting - haunting - fighting -
realizing - calming.
Sometimes I just write the word, "word".
It reminds me that my goal is to write words.
It could be at night.
It could be at a party.
It could be during sex.
It could be while taking a shit.
It could be when a kid walks
by with a blue backpack and
I am envious to see
that he has everything in the world to look forward to.
It could be the crusted toothpaste on the dude's lip.
It could be the smile my grandfather used to share.
It could be the rim of a trashcan.
It could be the scent of Indian food.
It could be because I have no other choice.
It could be because I feel I have too.
It could be any of these things.
And for writers, that is exactly how it should be.

When It Rains, Smoke Rises

Her tan jacket floated in front of me.
The light on the corner of 60th and Madison
gave the fabric its last breath of color.

She vanished behind the orange and white striped tube.
Out of the giant cigarette,
the street spewed smoke.

Higher and higher it rose.
The entire sky was foggy.

The beads collected on my shoulder.
The warm streets cooled.
The day's rush subsided.

I walked to the subway.
I had never seen such a purple sky.

I was ready to go home.
So too was New York City.

No matter how much you want to love someone,
you can't if they don't let you.

Ice Cream Truck Jingles

I woke up and kids were playing on my street.
The alarm clock rang in the form
of an ice cream truck.
"Shit!" I thought when I looked at my watch.
9:44.
"Damn it! I'm going to be late...again."
The night before, I went to bed to take a nap.
These naps always were intended to last an hour.
Sometimes they did, sometimes they didn't.
Sometimes they lasted until morning.
It wasn't uncommon for me to sleep
more than 12 hours:
7 to 7.
Large remnants of eye goo,
blamed on contact lenses,
told me if I had slept in too long.

So, as the ice cream clerk started serving vanilla and chocolate
twists
all I could wonder was, "Why is it so dark out?"
I assumed a storm was coming.
It seemed to rain every other hour this summer,
and the kids were out.
I snatched my phone.
Lord, what are all these text messages?
Everyone must be bored at work.
"Crap! get your ass up, Joe!"
I sprang from my bed.
Frantic, I ran to my shower.
"Should I even shower? Should I cab it?"
Time-travel scenarios ran through my head.
"If I get a cab now, I could make it by 10 a.m."
10 a.m. was normal for me,
and in this hysteria it seemed to be best to get to work ASAP.
I remembered that my boss was out on vacation.
"Hell, just shower, a quick rinse, man, and get out – make it by
10:30 and no one will know the difference."

Yeah, fuck it – make up an excuse if you need too.
I took one last look outside.
"Is there a solar eclipse?"
It was so damn dark outside.
Wait.
It was 10 p.m.
I dried off and laid back down.
I set my alarm.
Within 10 minutes, I couldn't hear anything.
All of the kids must have finished their ice creams.

As Memory Burns

The candle burns and the melody continues.
We keep living in it.
The wick is gone.
We hold on to the wax.
Crusted onto
the lantern
The glass
The table
our fingers.
And we listen
while the nostalgia repeats itself.
We sing along.

Incompetent Schemers

They knew I could do it,
but I didn't want to do it for them.
That didn't matter:
I had the juice.
They knew it, and they were waiting to drink.
They wouldn't right away.
They never dared to take sips.
Never would they taste some of the flavor
and learn from it.
They'd never try to go on with it alone.
Instead, they wait on their greatest asset
until the deadline crept uncomfortably close,
and although they have time,
they make every effort to appear busy.
Too flustered
Too stupid
Then, right as the end neared, they'd gulp my juice.
They'd use everything,
everything I'd practiced.
One swift gulp.
Gone
The worst part?
I never was told how good it was.
It was exactly like they'd planned:
nothing at all was said afterwards.
If they had said anything, then they'd have been caught,
So the schemers never said anything.

Art is purely about intention.
Its medium
is only a technicality.

Envy

From birth we're told we have something special.
Each year mounts more accolades.
Our confidence relies on feeling accomplished.
It's all about achievement.

All too soon the cheers become less frequent.
For some, it has been quiet for a long time.
First place hasn't happened for them.
And the truth is there is no knowing when the applause will
end... or start for that matter,
but when it's gone – when we're used to it...
We'll do anything to get it back.

As the years go by it may become insignificant.
Possibly you'll find your place in life.
But what about those that don't settle?
What about those that need to be heard?
Need to be witnessed.
Need to be sustained.

The manic inside all of us is waiting to roar,
and those you trust will diminish your importance.
They'll take it away if they envy your applause.
It's a battle.

Competition has never been about compassion.
It's ingrained in us,
just like when we were born.
We seek to hold on to it.
We want the most of it.
In the end we can become obsessed by it.

But it seems all too petty when it's stolen from us.
Envy is the root of all evil.
It has nothing to do with
money
clothes

houses
cars
things.

It's another scam in the end,
a trick bleeding with inferiority,
a blindside against yourself.
The mirage will only survive if you tolerate it.
I don't allow myself to do that anymore.
No, I know I'm good enough.
The cheers are not as important
as they used to be.

Everyone is Together When They're Alone

It's doesn't really matter,
I suppose,
whether I'm alone
or I think I am.
To be honest I prefer to be left alone,
but there are moments
when I consider letting in companionship.
Yet, even when someone is there,
I'm alone.
They are alone,
but we sit there,
talking the talk
drinking the drink.
Just for the moment we trick ourselves,
but even when we wake up together,
I choose to be alone.
My mind mingles between the thoughts
and decisions for the day.
I know she does the same.
So we lay there side by side.
All I have to do is look over,
but I don't right now.
I just want to be alone.

Writing When You Think You Have Nothing Left

Fatigue.

It is the goal sometimes.

It's there.

It's located in a place
where you have a little bit of energy,

just enough so that your
best and most stripped down ideas can finally be found.

In the midst of trying to escape life
and all of its uncertainties,
eccentricities
and periods of insecurity,
there's your life.
And your life,
my life,
everyone's life is so good.
It can be so good
even if it seems so damned.
It's not perfect,
it's so beautifully flawed,
but if you take it on,
if you believe in tomorrow,
it can be so good.
It can be so damn good.

The Sculpture Is Nothing But a Figment...
Of Someone Else's Imagination

Giving yourself to someone
seems to be our most favored topic of discussion.
We yearn for it.
We fear it.
We want it.

And maybe we shouldn't do it.
What's wrong with being alone?
Alone, where you can think for yourself,
where you can define yourself,
where you can be yourself.

I'm not ready to be a statue,
chiseled and designed by someone else,
made to look perfect,
made without noticeable imperfections.

I wonder about the inside of the statues,
their rawness.
I want to remove the sheen
and really see what's inside.
Those parts are rarely observed.

Most fear what they'll find,
that too much will be found out
about others
about you
about me
We might find something that causes us to leave.
I guess that's where all the madness comes from.
Leaving would mean being alone.
Maybe that's why we want to give ourselves up.
But why compromise your worth?

I'm okay with being alone.
I'm willing to be patient.
It scares me a little bit,
but I'm okay,
I am,
and you are too.

Stuck... Again

I can't stand the thought of being stuck.
Stuck in a lease.
Stuck in a relationship.
Stuck in a job.
Stuck writing this damn poem.

It probably explains why
I didn't go to graduate school.
It probably explains why
I worry for days, months, after a one-night stand.
It probably explains why
I'd rather write than be around people.
I'd rather not care at all;
it'd be safer that way.

But I care.
I care about all the ways in which I could be stuck.
And therefore I remain stuck.

I'm stuck with my anxieties.
I'm stuck with my former faults.
I'm stuck with allowing myself to laugh about the past.
I'm stuck with trying to love again.
I'm stuck with guilt.
I'm stuck with more guilt.
I'm stuck with the writing.
I'm stuck with being patient for a publication.
I'm stuck with fear that it won't happen.
I'm stuck with the fear that it will happen.
I'm stuck with dealing with my mind.
I'm stuck with the demons that
prevail from time to time.
I'm stuck with reminding myself to breathe.
I'm stuck with being stuck.

As much as anyone wants to
control their fate, it is for naught.

We're stuck with the inevitable
virtue of what life hands us.
There'll be days of luck.
There'll be days of hard times.
There'll be everything else in between.
You'll be stuck.
I'll be stuck.

Stuck has nothing to do with choices in life.
Life is a vicious cycle of choices we're stuck with.

And just like now,
just like in the future,
when our time has come,
we'll be left feeling stuck.

Man's Growl

I growl because I'm scared.
I fight because a small part of me hopes I lose.
It'd be easier then, 'cause at least
I wouldn't have known what comes after success.
If I lose, it'll be over,
and
I won't feel guilty for not trying,
but then I remember I'm the bear.
I'm not attuned to diffident tendencies.
No, it isn't that easy.
I'm impetuous, and my desires are rampant.
I can't help but thrive on ambition.
I am motivated by the small leaks of hope.
I see each opponent as an opportunity to fight again.
And this time,
I'm ready to win.

Whether the flame
or its shadow,
eventually,
everyone meets the ashes.

Time Wasted

Do something great with your time.
Don't sit and play on your phone,
or watch television.
Create an idea.
Read.
Yes, read anything.
Get the dictionary and read.
Read the names of streets.
I see people and they tap the screens of their phones.
They swipe in the same motion
as flipping pages in a book.
They're puppets, indulged by
the innovators of distraction,
wasted.
So much more could be done
if only a small percentage of time was used better.
What drives these Motherfuckers?
Really?
Candy Crush?
Complaining also fills the void.
Resentment
Isolation
Vanity
Periodic moments of inspiration
quickly subdued by fear
that it's not worth my time
or that it's too hard.
"I'll never get it done!"
What ever happened to belief?
What ever happened to taking a chance?
I ride with the delusional ones,
Obsessed
Crazed by the lack of substance.
Ones who fucking feel!
Ones who give a shit.
Ones that use their time productively.
Ones that don't need to read this poem.
I don't know.

Maybe even this was a waste of time?
You know what...
I have better things to do.

Normal Beauty

The beauty you seek is in -
The streets you walk.
The smiles you share.
The smiles you don't expect.
The isolation of thoughts.
The tears you shed.
The words you read.
The times you hate.
The times you love.
The disgust you'd rather be rid of.
The car you beat while crossing the road.
The sound of nothing.
The note needed to ease the day.
The change you've been waiting for.
The days that shouldn't end.
The days that should.
The rarity in experiencing the extraordinary.
The overwhelming abundance in being normal.

Because being normal
is beautiful.

Let My Mind Speak

Writing isn't when thought and memory collide.
If it were easy,
everyone would be walking around
with a pen and notebook.

Most people don't care.
They'd rather not take on the burden.
They don't dare take a look into their soul.
Those are the complacent ones.
I envy them.

My mind is too damn stubborn.
It races because I've allowed it too.
And in between
drinking
fucking
and wasting my thoughts on other trivial escapes...
I write

We speak to each other
and just like everyone else
we want our voices heard.
I get so damn depressed
when I can't take a moment with my mind.

But sometimes I shut up.
At other times my mind shuts up.
And when either one of us listens,
my hand records.

My mind is talking right now.
So don't call me.
I'm taking down some notes.
I don't want to miss out on what my mind is saying.

I feel free at 2am,
when the cab drives over
Queensboro Bridge.
I lean out the window and yell,
I scream so loud.
I'm not scared,
I just need this.
It's the only opportunity I'll have
until next Saturday.

Enough Said
Don't think,
just feel.

Pull The Pin

She thought I had the upper hand,
but she did.
I couldn't be around someone as amazing as her.
That would be too caustic for me.
All I can remember is the length of her legs.
I still think about those legs.
My hand inside them.
And when she grabbed my right shoulder tightly,
warning me that it was too much,
I feared I might have been hurting her.
But I wasn't.
She wanted it.
I loved giving it to her.
Every push seemed better than the last.
She breathed so elegantly.
Her lungs were so full.
She was alive and I felt as if I was saving her.
I couldn't take that responsibility.
It's a lot of pressure for a man.
Yeah, we can act like we don't care,
or like you're just some piece,
but when we know it's right,
we run,
we want out.
The soul is a ticking hand grenade.
As much as we let our partners hold its pin,
we know the looming danger.
So before someone challenges us,
we leave,
acting oblivious to the moment's serenity,
leaving,
to roam the city as hyenas.
Yelling, amusing ourselves.
Women don't get it.
We don't have the power.
They do.
But we only admit that.
Once we know.
They won't pull the pin.

Reach

So low
and
down in the dirt
that even the sight of a ladder would make you cry
'cause the hole
is too low.
It's impossible to get out.
Time
Patience
An inner strength that comes from nearly quitting.
I relate to people feeling like this.
I doubt asking for a handout
raises anyone's confidence.
But who's to say?
The degradation can bring you so low.
It can snatch the last morsels of self-esteem.
But hold on.
Hold it.
Never will you feel this again.
Especially if you don't let the others get to you.
Strength comes from those who refuse to give up,
and worth comes
from those who believe in
a better day
a lighter day
a day where the rain washes away everything,
when jumping is the only thing that your legs do,
when you reach so high,
higher than a place you thought possible
higher than a place you knew existed.
It's there,
it's waiting for you.

We deal with the dealt deck
by bluffing until we break even.

Ambivalent Lust And Then... Nothing

I thought this was over,
but it happened.
It was strange to experience it again.
I woke up
with your arms
fitting like they were supposed to.

I left wondering –
Was I hoping for more?
But there was nothing.
It was just like before.
It really sucks when that happens.
There is nothing you can do.
A vulnerable state of anticipation.
Questions meddle in the mind.
Thoughts that had dissipated recur.
Feelings turn fickle by questioning romanticism.
That seems to be the general course of things.
It could go in any direction.
There is a small opening.
I'm scared to pursue it.
It may feel right, but my past hinders me.
It prevents me from moving forward

When it was time to depart, we didn't say anything.
Just like the last time.
It was nothing.
It would be nothing.
It will be nothing.
Well, it won't... until I give the moment a try again.

Hartford Bound

The bus stops - goes - stops - waits.
The sky turns blue, grey and black.
Everyone's trying to get somewhere.
The family
A girlfriend
A new job
Some are just trying to go,
no destination in mind.
Nomads
on another trip,
another place,
anywhere but here.

Strollers

The worst part about being a dad in NYC?
It has to be carrying a stroller up the subway stairs.
When I think of being a dad,
that's what I think of first,
having to lug it around and through turnstiles
while passengers look at you thinking,
"Come on, guy, take a cab!"
"What are you trying to prove?"
"What? Do you think you're a good dad or something?"
"Yeah, really?"
I don't know.
It only looks like they're carrying a stroller.
I guess I should give them a break,
'cause that's what you're supposed to do.

The words we write
tend to be better
than the ones we speak.

Most Steps Will Be Unbalanced

The road can appear slippery even when it's dry out.
Sometimes directions aren't as clear
as we'd like them to be.
But
we keep walking.
Yes – well, we should keep walking,
no matter how many times we fall.
Aside from all the mistakes, mishaps and misfortune,
we'd rather – no we must – keep moving.

Once we find success,
we don't think about slipping,
but we will:
around every corner of success
is a road waiting.
It's full of agony and despair.

No wonder.
I've seen too many men wait for the road to clear.
Seeing a fabricated slippery road ahead,
they wait until it appears clear.
A cautious mind is a mad one.

It's a sad day when someone stops.
In the end he'll wish to Hell he'd kept moving.
It's a damn shame.
He can only blame himself,
but he'll blame the streets forever.

Aussie Girl And Frank

The Aussie girl fawned over Frank.
His looks were enough for her.
I remember when my looks were enough.
The hair is fading,
the belly is a bit more rotund.
Working out is no longer a hobby.
It has become a necessity,
a way of keeping up appearances.
Otherwise they'll rapidly dwindle,
like they have since 28.
Perhaps it's just a moment of animosity.
Those happen.
But tomorrow I'll go to the gym.
Or, fuck it:
Maybe I'll just write.
Frank doesn't do that at all.

Pull It Together

Decreed by loneliness,
it's about finding ways not to be alone.
We strive to be in a community.
Love itself is used as security,
a way to confirm that we aren't alone.
But we are alone - even when we are surrounded.
That is something we cannot change,
just like pebbles in a stream
or a strand of grass in a field.
Each component is alone.
Beautifully segmented.
We shouldn't try to be anything
but
ourselves.

Only the wild ones
are bold enough
to take on
the immensity of it all.

A Stream Of Consciousness Should Be Dry At Times

This morning's rise was the purest one yet.
There should have been nothing but glory today.
Last evening was perfect – she was perfect.
Perfect.

I was flawed.
I was just as flawed as usual.
And she listened as
I tapped the bar's counter.
I had a breakthrough.
I was anxious.
Not because I wanted to be anxious,
but because she understood how anxious
I was, about my work... about her.

Tap
Tap
Tap
The mumbles turned into words of nonsense.
My shortcomings and visions of tomorrow
blended by the anticipation of her,
of everything that would've been great,
but I didn't know how to handle it.

We left in a good place.
We left together.
We left in a good place.
"We."
It's nice to say that.
It seems harder and harder to say that.
Being together doesn't happen enough.
When it does it can be difficult to handle.

I wish I could have placed it in a bottle,
a time capsule of purity,
a detour from the mix of insecurities.
That's what I thought then.
That's what I looked for.
That's what we all look for.

But back at her place,
the jitter was there,
The confusion was unnerving.
It all had to do with everything and nothing.
It all resided in my head.

I didn't want to deal with it.
I wanted to escape.
I didn't want to be there.
I didn't want to mess this up.
I didn't.
No, I hope she knows, I never wanted to mess this up.

This is something that only the dreamers can experience.
Destined for the beauty of peace,
the mind can finally sleep
without the pressure of the world,
of past experiences,
of influences,
of everything unto itself.

The barrage of self-doubt is a deadly beast.
It can sting.
It can ruin the beauty of life.
It can be misconstrued.
It can.
It really can.

The next morning it was clearly apparent.
There were mishaps.
I had regrets.
And the sad thing is that there did not have to be.
The damn drink.
We rushed and it was confusing.

I had ruined the beauty in everything.
The stain had left something more memorable.
What should have never been forgotten
was the first to exit.

That's the sadness of most things.
That's the problem with it all.
It all comes down to the things
that shouldn't be remembered.
The moments where we lose our inhibitions.
The times that we should not dwell
on the casualties of our actions.
But those are the times we remember most.
Not because we want to,
but because they affect us most.

So we dwell.
We wonder.
We regret.
We hope.
We wish.
We want.
We desire.
We ... well we just sit.
We sit and think.

And wonder if things can change.
If hope is something more cerebral than a fantasy.
Maybe things can come back to the light,
where we can believe that the truth
really will set us free.

That the inhibitions of flaws will move us forward.
People will look at us for who we are,
and not for mistakes we've made.
They will see us in a pure moment, and not in one influenced by
the things we may have done or said.

To know oneself is the biggest challenge.
It is something we strive to find,
but it takes forever to truly find out.
It does, doesn't it?

And that's okay,
because we aren't simple.
We are complex.
Everything is truncated by the existence
of something preceding it.
The past is a beast that bites us in times of hope.
It is the time that limits our abilities
and halts our progress.
It's grueling – it is – every part of it.

But I wish I could be with her.
The interaction,
the time of solace,
it was all there,
but that can't be seen:
it was blurred.
Maybe it will never be clear.

I know the look of something as real as a tepid fawn yearning on
the expectation that something will last.
Even if she is scared shitless.
Even if she doesn't want to let herself
think it will be possible.
Even if the previous damage is there.
Even if...

I suppose that's the basis for all of this -
The 'if'
The chance
The possibility
And that is where I know there's a possibility.

If I believe in it,
if I really want it
I can make it happen.
Nothing else matters.

It all comes from the burning surge
of coal that flitters inside.
It's there,
it's always there,
and it will flare,
it will flame,
and it is up to us to let it.
Even when the chill seems to subdue,
we must believe in the flame.

I watch it.
I hope that she does too
I hope...
But even if she doesn't,
I feel fortunate knowing it could spark.
It's been cold in my belly.
I wish the fire could blaze again.
Maybe if she can see it my way,
it will blaze again.

Hope is all we have.
It's a carnival ticket, man.
It's typically a bad deal,
but every so often,
when you least expect it,
it turns out to be the best experience of your life.

Those are the times I think of.
The moments of hope.
The moments of subtle fear infused with purity.
That's what I think of.
I just hope.
I do.
I hope she can too one day.

She has every capability.
I have every opportunity to mess it up.
I refuse this time.
I do.
No, this time I'm going to try.
This time I'm letting it flare.
This time I believe in it.
This time.
With her.
Her.
Just
her.

The Struggle Isn't Real

Everyone wants to commiserate.
Everyone needs to have a story.
Something to validate the value of their lives.
Without it, their success doesn't seem to be as deserved.
It's only an expectation,
and not what they worked for.

Coffee Breaks

I'd rather be delusional than disdained.
Everything is temporary –
even this coffee will end soon –
the subway sandwich –
the I Love NY t-shirt...
Packaged by distraction –
making apps to distract us.
Progress is halted by the inability
that we distract ourselves with.
Staring into strangers.
Taking a guess.
Wanting to see more in them than ourselves.
Assuming they have more going on.
Scared that we aren't living up to our potential.
Sip.
Add a little more sugar.
Get back to reality, just like everyone else.

No matter if you win or lose, a piece of you is erased.

A Beautiful Pie Crust

A victor of looks,
a strong jawline with washboard abs.
A victim of vanity.
Plump, chinless with a rim around the center.
There is nothing worse than being good looking,
whatever the hell that really means.
People rely on it.
Some plead for it.
It is a desperate, sorrowful sight,

a crutch that crumbles with time,
denial that
aggrandizes until the grave.
We earnestly seek ways to pursue
the vanity of the past.
We are locked in a lasting struggle
to re-vamp the allure that means...
nothing.

A life based on subjectivity.
An opinion on appearances.
A compromise.
A misconception.
A flaw.

We are impressed by those that feel lower
than the most horrid faces out there.
We are surrounded
by distraction,
by meager minds
and by empty souls.
Lost souls.
Wanting souls.
Wanting something, yearning for anything.
Wishing they had something to offer
other than a lovely face,
clean, pure and without scars.
Just emptiness

based on a flavorless story.
A pie's crust in need of filling.
Tastelessly needing just a little more.

I Wear The Shame

In our ways we get by.
We all deal with it,
a lingering feeling of disappointment
like a barnacle on a sea rock.
We forget about it.
Our façade is changed by it,
the unspoken shame of the past,
the regret of it,
the admiration for those who
have gone through it too.

It might happen again.

You may have to see the faces of doubt.
You may have to face yours in the morning.
That is the worst part about it,
wondering.
We all wear the past's shame.
How will you disguise it?

Freedom

Red Fox Runs

There's a red fox that follows me.
Nobody else can see him.
I don't talk about the fox too much.
I'd suspect if I did, others would call me wild.
But the red fox watches me.
Even on the snowiest days
I can see his red fur through
the precipitating flakes of glory.

We never see eye to eye.
He snarls at me from time to time,
especially when he senses my vulnerability.
He probably believes I'll quit.
He probably thinks I'll forget about him.
But I never allow myself to get too low.
No, if I did that,
the red fox might leave.
I can't let that happen:
he needs to watch over me.

Sometimes I try to get the best of him,
but as swift as his tail whips at the lightest touch,
he runs.
He does this on purpose.
He only allows me a temporary grasp,
a short-lived glimpse of perfect purity.

I see myself as the red fox runs.
He keeps me hunting.
I know I'll catch him one day.

Love is a beautiful mistake.

Photo: Ryan Marcus

The Author

Joseph Adam Lee writes like a man with his back against the wall. A Franco-American from the mill town of Lewiston, Maine, he carries the scars of the working class into every line. Now raising hell in New York City, he drinks, he writes, he bleeds— because no gatekeeper ever handed him permission.

Contact Information

Email: joe@therebelwithin.com
Website: www.josephadamlee.com
Instagram: @joseph.adam.lee

Letters & Packages

Red Fox Runs Press
C/O Joseph Adam Lee
909 3rd Avenue
#127
New York, New York 10150